3.60

THEMES IN CANADIAN LITERATURE
General Editor *David Arnason*

P9-EEA-110

The Frontier Experience

Edited by
Jack Hodgins

Macmillan of Canada

ISBN 0-7705-1264-X

Themes in Canadian Literature

The Urban Experience edited by John Stevens
The Maritime Experience edited by Michael O. Nowlan
The Frontier Experience edited by Jack Hodgins
The Prairie Experience edited by Terry Angus
Isolation in Canadian Literature edited by David Arnason and
    Alice K. Hale
The Immigrant Experience edited by Leuba Bailey
Native Peoples in Canadian Literature edited by William and
    Christine Mowat
The Artist in Canadian Literature edited by Lionel Wilson
The Search for Identity edited by James Foley
The Role of Woman in Canadian Literature edited by Elizabeth
    McCullough
Canadian Humour and Satire edited by Theresa Ford

Other titles in preparation

Printed in Canada

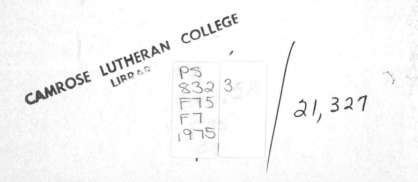

ACKNOWLEDGMENTS

Grateful acknowledgment is made for the use of copyright material.

Photographs: p. 3, Ontario Ministry of Natural Resources; p. 12, Ontario Ministry of the Environment; p. 23, Public Archives of Canada; p. 29, death photo of Albert Johnson, Glenbow-Alberta Institute; p. 44, St. Elias Range, Yukon Territory, Miller Services Ltd.; p. 55, Ontario Ministry of the Environment; p. 68, Canadian Pulp and Paper Association (Malak); p. 82, Canadian Pacific Railway Company; p. 90, Miller Services Ltd.; p. 104, USAF.

Margaret Atwood: "The Animals in That Country" and "Progressive Insanities of a Pioneer" from *The Animals in That Country* by Margaret Atwood, reprinted by permission of Oxford University Press (Canada).
Will R. Bird: "The Movies Come to Gull Point" from *Sunrise for Peter and Other Stories* by Will R. Bird, reprinted by permission of the Author.
Earle Birney: "Bushed" from *Collected Poems* by Earle Birney, reprinted by permission of McClelland and Stewart Limited, Toronto.
Emily Carr: "An Artist's Tabernacle" from *Hundreds and Thousands: The Journals of Emily Carr*, ©1966 by Clarke, Irwin & Company Limited. Used by permission.
Dave Godfrey: "River Two Blind Jacks", originally published in *Tamarack Review*, reprinted by permission of the Author.
Hugh Hood: "After the Sirens" from *Flying a Red Kite* by Hugh Hood, reprinted by permission of McGraw-Hill Ryerson Limited.
Douglas LePan: "Canoe-Trip" from *The Wounded Prince and Other Poems* by Douglas LePan, Chatto and Windus (1948). Used by permission.
Charles Lillard: "Quixote in the Snow" from *Contemporary Poetry of British Columbia*, reprinted by permission of Sono Nis Press.
Gwendolyn MacEwen: "Dark Pines Under Water" from *The Shadow-Maker* by Gwendolyn MacEwen, reprinted by permission of The Macmillan Company of Canada Limited.
Thomas William Magrath: "Bear-Hunting In Upper Canada" from *Authentic Letters from Upper Canada*, edited by Thomas Radcliff, The Macmillan Company of Canada Limited.
Susanna Moodie: "The Settling of Tom Wilson" from *Roughing It in the Bush* by Susanna Moodie (1852).
Farley Mowat: "Tundra" from *Maclean's* Magazine, May 1973, reprinted by permission of McClelland and Stewart Limited, Toronto.
John Newlove: "Ride Off Any Horizon" from *Black Night Window* by John Newlove, reprinted by permission of McClelland and Stewart Limited, Toronto.
E. J. Pratt: "Brébeuf's Last Journey" from "Brébeuf and His Brethren" from *The*

CONTENTS

INTRODUCTION: Deeper Into the Forest

Coureurs de bois . . . Perhaps in the history of Canada no image has had more power to fire the imagination than that of those reckless "runners of the woods", setting off in their canoes to penetrate the largely unexplored and unexplained vast wildernesses of the continent. The impulse both to experience and to celebrate the journey into unknown territory has sponsored the creation of a good deal of our literature in the past and continues to do so today. It is an experience not far removed from any of us, living in a country where the wilderness is never very distant and where some of our pioneers are living still. There is room here for us to get away from one another and even, if we desire, to strike off entirely on our own into private landscapes. And if we choose to stay at home we can still relate meaningfully to a body of literature which records, celebrates, and mythologizes the experience of going out into unknown regions, encountering the frontier.

The frontier, if we consider the origin of the word, is quite literally a forehead, and a forehead in one sense is what separates us "in here" from all the rest of the less familiar world "out there". Dictionaries expand the meaning of the word to describe the beginnings of the wilds, the border of a country, and an uncertain or undeveloped field of knowledge. Critic John Moss, examining the literature of Canada in *Patterns of Isolation,* describes the frontier as an alternative to conventional society: "It is a place of flight and of discovery, a condition of individual being, in the struggle to endure." Many of our writers have chosen to separate themselves from society and to live alone; even more are fascinated to explore in their writing the effects of this experience on the individual. This anthology attempts to demonstrate the variety of the literature which comes from "out there" in the "place of flight and of discovery".

There is something in the nature of man which has kept him seeking in this country the new Eden, which has moved him gradually from right to left across the map, stopping only long enough to discover that what he'd sought was less than paradise after all and full of dangers. Taming it only resulted in a reproduction of the garrison society he'd left behind. Not even the Pacific coast reduced him to frustration; he turned northward into colder landscapes or, remaining in one of the thousands of ex-frontiers

1

across the land, turned to explorations of less obvious frontiers, the exciting geography of mind/soul: science, art, religion, the future.

The selections in this book have been chosen to represent the Canadian response to the frontier experience. Through poems, short stories, and essays, writers attempt to find some kind of meaning in the search for Eden, the encounter with the wilderness, the disappointment that follows the reaching of the goal. When he leaves society and goes "deeper into the forest", whether to escape the law or to find himself, to establish a dynasty or to search for peace, to exploit the natural resources or to survive the holocaust, always he discovers unknown forces that bend his attention back, inevitably, on himself. Thus, Birney's hermit locks himself into the very solitude which has driven him mad with fear. Emily Carr, on the other hand, approaches the wilderness as a place of worship; the self she encounters is a part of the natural world and, moreover, a harmonious part of the universe.

The first six selections in the book treat their subject in a very direct way: author confronts frontier and tells what he discovers. The writers of the next nine selections, however, use frontier experiences as raw material from which they shape artistic works: the true story of the Jesuit missionary is told by E. J. Pratt with the traditional devices of the literary epic; the historical facts of the tracking of the "Red River Trapper" are borrowed and shaped by Rudy Wiebe into an unusual and powerful short story. The final group of writers explores new frontiers: the north, the human mind, the future, even death—the frontier for which, perhaps, all the others may be only symbols or unacknowledged reminders.

Since the primary purpose of this collection is enjoyment and enlightenment, the questions section is intended to enhance rather than detract from the reading experience. It is hoped that here, as in the rest of the book, will be found ideas for fruitful discussion, enthusiastic research, and original writing. The excited exploration of a literary theme growing out of a small collection of pieces like this does not end; rather, it leaves the page and rapidly gathers other pages and other people and goes on expanding and deepening for as long and as far as anyone has the imagination and desire to follow it.

Jack Hodgins

THE ANIMALS IN THAT COUNTRY
Margaret Atwood

In that country the animals
have the faces of people:

the ceremonial
cats possessing the streets

the fox run
politely to earth, the huntsmen
standing around him, fixed
in their tapestry of manners

the bull, embroidered
with blood and given
an elegant death, trumpets, his name
stamped on him, heraldic brand
because

(when he rolled
on the sand, sword in his heart, the teeth
in his blue mouth were human)

he is really a man

even the wolves, holding resonant
conversations in their
forests thickened with legend.

　　　In this country the animals
　　　have the faces of
　　　animals.

　　　Their eyes
　　　flash once in car headlights
　　　and are gone.

　　　Their deaths are not elegant.

　　　They have the faces of
　　　no-one.

LAURENTIAN SHIELD
F. R. Scott

Hidden in wonder and snow, or sudden with summer,
This land stares at the sun in a huge silence
Endlessly repeating something we cannot hear.
Inarticulate, arctic,
Not written on by history, empty as paper,
It leans away from the world with songs in its lakes
Older than love, and lost in the miles.

This waiting is wanting.
It will choose its language
When it has chosen its technic,
A tongue to shape the vowels of its productivity.

A *language of flesh and of roses.*

Now there are pre-words,
Cabin syllables,
Nouns of settlement
Slowly forming, with steel syntax,
The long sentence of its exploitation.

The first cry was the hunter, hungry for fur,
And the digger for gold, nomad, no-man, a particle;
Then the bold commands of monopoly, big with machines,
Carving its kingdoms out of the public wealth;
And now the drone of the plane, scouting the ice,
Fills all the emptiness with neighbourhood
And links our future over the vanished pole.

But a deeper note is sounding, heard in the mines,
The scattered camps and the mills, a language of life,
And what will be written in the full culture of occupation
Will come, presently, tomorrow,
From millions whose hands can turn this rock into children.

RIDE OFF ANY HORIZON
John Newlove

Ride off any horizon
and let the measure fall
where it may —

on the hot wheat,
on the dark yellow fields
of wild mustard, the fields

of bad farmers, on the river,
on the dirty river full
of boys and on the throbbing

powerhouse and the low dam
of cheap cement and rocks
boiling with white water,

and on the cows and their powerful
bulls, the heavy tracks
filling with liquid at the edge

of the narrow prairie
river running steadily away.

*

Ride off any horizon
and let the measure fall
where it may —

among the piles of bones
that dot the prairie

in vision and history
(the buffalo and deer,

dead indians, dead settlers
the frames of lost houses

left behind in the dust
of the depression,

dry and profound, that
will come again in the land

and in the spirit, the land
shifting and the minds

blown dry and empty —
I have not seen it! except

in pictures and talk —
but there is the fence

covered with dust, laden,
the wrecked house stupidly empty) —

here is a picture for your wallet,
of the beaten farmer and his wife
leaning toward each other —

sadly smiling, and emptied of desire.

*

Ride off any horizon
and let the measure fall
where it may —

off the edge
of the black prairie

as you thought you could fall,
a boy at sunset

not watching the sun
set but watching the black earth,

never-ending they said in school,
round: but you saw it ending,

finished, definite, precise —
visible only miles away.

*

Ride off any horizon
and let the measure fall
where it may —

on a hot night the town
is in the streets —

the boys and girls
are practising against

each other, the men
talk and eye the girls —

the women talk and
eye each other, the indians
play pool: eye on the ball.

*

Ride off any horizon
and let the measure fall
where it may —

and damn the troops, the horsemen
are wheeling in the sunshine,
the cree, practising

for their deaths: mr poundmaker,
gentle sweet mr bigbear,
it is not unfortunately

quite enough to be innocent,
it is not enough merely
not to offend —

at times to be born
is enough, to be
in the way is too much —

some colonel otter, some
major-general middleton will
get you, you —

indian. It is no good to say,
I would rather die
at once than be in that place —

though you love that land more,
you will go where they take you.

*

Ride off any horizon
and let the measure fall —

where it may;
it doesn't have to be

the prairie. It could be
the cold soul of the cities
blown empty by commerce

and desiring commerce
to fill up emptiness.

The streets are full of people.

It is night, the lights
are on; the wind

blows as far as it may. The streets
are dark and full of people.

Their eyes are fixed as far as
they can see beyond each other —

to the concrete horizon, definite,
tall against the mountains,
stopping vision visibly.

BEAR-HUNTING IN UPPER CANADA
Thomas William Magrath

From Thos. Wm. Magrath, Esq., Upper Canada,
to the Rev. Thomas Radcliff, Dublin.

Erindale, January, 1832.

My dear Sir,

I follow up, at your desire, the particulars of the *field* or rather *forest* sports — and having closed my last long letter, with the subject of deer hunting, I will commence this with another description of amusement.

Bear Shooting

The bear, though apparently an unwieldy animal, gets over the ground, faster than one could suppose.

I have had a pet one for years, (reared from a cub) that follows me about, and has often kept up with my horse, when at a round canter.

This huge black bear, standing five feet high when upright, is of the *fair* sex. The name to which she answers, "Mocaunse".* Her qualities, mildness and docility.

She runs about the house like a dog, and is invited to the drawing-room, when any visitor arrives who wishes to make her acquaintance — when my avocations led me to the woods in distant parts of the province, Mocaunse was the companion of my journey, and the nightly guardian of my tent — not a sound or stir could be made, without a warning from her cautionary whine, or growl.

It was amusing to observe with what gravity she took her seat each morning at the opposite side of the mat, upon which my breakfast was arranged, and the *patience* with which she waited for her share of the repast. In this cardinal virtue she failed but in one instance. One morning on the shore of Lake-Huron, my party having stopped to prepare breakfast, whilst my servant was getting ready mine, I plunged into the lake to indulge in a bracing swim, and on returning with

* Mo caunse is, in the Mississagua language, Young Bear.

"encrease of appetite", found Miss Mocaunse, lying down perfectly at her ease, having devoured every morsel of my breakfast — biscuit, bread, sugar, &c. all eaten up, and the tea *equipage,* &c. &c., in the most glorious confusion!! Conceiving it necessary to impress strongly on her recollection my disapprobation of such unladylike conduct, and to guard against the recurrence of a similar disaster, I tied her to a post and bestowed on her hairy sides so sound a drubbing, that benefitting by this practical lecture upon patience, Mocaunse has invariably waited breakfast for me ever since.

Bears are not as numerous as they were on our first coming to Canada — nor are they as troublesome, or as dangerous, as is supposed.

They have been sometimes known to carry off a small pig; but as to their attacking the human species, without being grievously provoked, (though it *may* have occurred,) no instance of it has come within my knowledge or experience. They seem rather to avoid a conflict with man, but if assailed and injured by him, there can be no doubt that his danger would be in proportion to their strength and power, which are very great.

The manner of shooting bears is much the same as in the case of deer, with the exception of using a heavier ball; and, that should you wound one badly without killing him, the sooner you get up a tree, too slight for *him* to climb, the better for your own security.

The Winter skin of the bear generally sells for six or seven dollars, and is very useful in sleighs, and as bedding.

The meat of a *young* bear is not unlike pork, but infinitely better. I have frequently eaten it, and like it. In New York it is considered a great delicacy, light, wholesome, and easily digested.

The interior fat, entitled *Bear's Grease,* is valuable for the hair, more in *demand,* than in *real existence,* in the shops.

I sent over some to ladies of my acquaintance, who perceiving that it was neither bleached nor scented, preferred, as I am told, the medicated hogslard of the perfumers.

One fellow that I shot, produced me as much pomatum as would cover the tonsured heads of an entire monastery, with a pile of hair as thick as a wig. I shall never, the longest day I live, forget the hour I killed him. It was one of my earliest essays in this branch of sporting.

A few weeks after we arrived at Toronto, my brother and I, in walking through the woods with our rifles, observed several pieces of bark falling to the ground from an old pine of great

dimensions, and on looking up, perceived an enormous bear, endeavouring to lodge himself in the hollow of the tree; after some consideration, it was agreed that *I* should be the assailant, my brother reserving his fire, lest mine should prove ineffectual. With this counter security against the *fraternal embrace* of a savage animal, dangerous when attacked, and furious when wounded, I took the most deliberate aim, and fired; at the moment came rolling to the ground "with hideous yell", the shaggy monster, writhing in agony.

We looked from him to each other — our resolve was rapid, as mutual — we ran for our lives; whichever occasionally took the lead, fancied the footsteps of the other, those of the pursuing bear; to our ear, he seemed to close upon us. The rustling of the underwood encreasing our alarm, doubled our speed; and it is difficult to say when we should have stopped, had we not found ourselves up to the knees in a deepening swamp. From hence we cast an anxious look behind, and not espying Bruin, plucked up our courage, and with my rifle re-loaded, and both cocked, began to retrace our steps, with due and exemplary caution; about midway a black squirrel darted across, our imaginations were so deeply occupied with terror of the bear, our rifles were in a second at our shoulders, and I will not say whether a little more would not have given us a second race.

We proceeded, however, *gallantly* towards the place where my first shot had taken effect, and making our observations at *respectful distance,* we remarked the bear at the foot of the same old pine; when, my brother, saying that he looked *suspicious,* fired with a certain aim; he need not have been so particular, as poor Bruin never winced, and had never moved from the moment that his terrifying, but expiring, roar had put us to ignominious flight.

Many a weary tug it cost us, to bring him to our house; where the candid confession of our exploits excited no inconsiderable fun and merriment.

THE SETTLING OF TOM WILSON
Susanna Moodie

We left the British shores on the 1st of July, and cast anchor, as I have already shown, under the Castle of St. Louis, at Quebec, on the 2nd of September, 1832. Tom Wilson sailed the 1st of May, and had a speedy passage, and was, as we heard from his friends, comfortably settled in the bush, had bought a farm, and meant to commence operations in the fall. All this was good news, and as he was settled near my brother's location, we congratulated ourselves that our eccentric friend had found a home in the wilderness at last, and that we should soon see him again.

On the 9th of September, the steamboat *William IV* landed us at the then small but rising town of —— , on Lake Ontario. The night was dark and rainy; the boat was crowded with emigrants; and when we arrived at the inn, we learnt that there was no room for us — not a bed to be had; nor was it likely, owing to the number of strangers that had arrived for several weeks, that we could obtain one by searching farther. Moodie requested the use of a sofa for me during the night; but even that produced a demur from the landlord. Whilst I awaited the result in a passage crowded with strange faces, a pair of eyes glanced upon me through the throng. Was it possible? — could it be Tom Wilson? Did any other human being possess such eyes, or use them in such an eccentric manner? In another second he had pushed his way to my side, whispering in my ear, "We met, 'twas in a crowd."

"Tom Wilson, is that you?"

"Do you doubt it? I flatter myself that there is no likeness of such a handsome fellow to be found in the world. It is I, I swear! — although very little of me is left to swear by. The best part of me I have left to fatten the mosquitoes and black flies in that infernal bush. But where is Moodie?"

"There he is—trying to induce Mr. S—, for love or money, to let me have a bed for the night."

"You shall have mine," said Tom. "I can sleep upon the floor of the parlour in a blanket, Indian fashion. It's a bargain

— I'll go and settle it with the Yankee directly; he's the best fellow in the world! In the meanwhile here is a little parlour, which is a joint-stock affair between some of us young hopefuls for the time being. Step in here, and I will go for Moodie. I long to tell him what I think of this confounded country. But you will find it out all in good time," and, rubbing his hands together with a most lively and mischievous expression, he shouldered his way through trunks, and boxes, and anxious faces, to communicate to my husband the arrangement he had so kindly made for us.

"Accept this gentleman's offer, sir, till tomorrow," said Mr. S —; "I can then make more comfortable arrangements for your family. But we are crowded — crowded to excess. My wife and daughters are obliged to sleep in a little chamber over the stable, to give our guests more room. Hard that, I guess, for decent people to locate over the horses."

These matters settled, Moodie returned with Tom Wilson to the little parlour, in which I had already made myself at home.

"Well, now, is it not funny that I should be the first to welcome you to Canada?" said Tom.

"But what are you doing here, my dear fellow?"

"Shaking every day with the ague. But I could laugh in spite of my teeth to hear them make such a confounded rattling; you would think they were all quarrelling which should first get out of my mouth. This shaking mania forms one of the chief attractions of this new country."

"I fear," said I, remarking how thin and pale he had become, "that this climate cannot agree with you."

"Nor I with the climate. Well, we shall soon be quits, for, to let you into a secret, I am now on my way to England."

"Impossible!"

"It is true."

"And the farm — what have you done with it?"

"Sold it."

"And your outfit?"

"Sold that too."

"To whom?"

"To one who will take better care of both than I did. Ah! such a country! — such people! — such rogues! It beats Australia hollow: you know your customers there — but here you have to find them out. Such a take-in! — God forgive them! I never could take care of money; and, one way or other, they have cheated me out of all mine. I have scarcely enough left to pay my passage home. But, to provide against the worst, I have bought a young bear, a splendid fellow, to make my peace with my uncle. You must see him; he is close by in the stable."

"Tomorrow we will pay a visit to Bruin; but tonight do tell us something about yourself, and your residence in the bush."

"You will know enough about the bush by-and-by. I am a bad historian," he continued, stretching out his legs, and yawning horribly, "a worse biographer. I never can find words to relate facts. But I will try what I can do. Mind, don't laugh at my blunders."

We promised to be serious — no easy matter while looking at and listening to Tom Wilson; and he gave us, at detached intervals, the following account of himself:

"My troubles began at sea. We had a fair voyage, and all that; but my poor dog, my beautiful Duchess! — that beauty in the beast — died. I wanted to read the funeral service over her, but the captain interfered — the brute! — and threatened to throw me into the sea along with the dead bitch, as the unmannerly ruffian persisted in calling my canine friend. I never spoke to him again during the rest of the voyage. Nothing happened worth relating until I got to this place, where I chanced to meet a friend who knew your brother, and I went up with him to the woods. Most of the wise men of Gotham we met on the road were bound to the woods; so I felt happy that I was, at least, in the fashion. Mr. —— was very kind, and spoke in raptures of the woods, which formed the theme of conversation during our journey — their beauty, their vastness, the comfort and independence enjoyed by those who had settled in them; and he so inspired me with the subject that I did nothing all day but sing as we rode along —

'A *life in the woods for me*',

until we came to the woods, and then I soon learned to sing that same, as the Irishman says, on the other side of my mouth."

Here succeeded a long pause, during which friend Tom seemed mightily tickled with his reminiscences, for he leaned back in his chair, and, from time to time, gave way to loud, hollow bursts of laughter.

"Tom, Tom! are you going mad?" said my husband, shaking him.

"I never was sane, that I know of," returned he. "You know that it runs in the family. But do let me have my laugh out. The woods! Ha! ha! When I used to be roaming through those woods, shooting — though not a thing could I ever find to shoot, for birds and beasts are not such fools as our English emigrants — and I chanced to think of you coming to spend the rest of your lives in the woods — I used to stop, and hold my sides, and laugh until the woods rang again. It was the only consolation I had."

"Good heavens!" said I, "let us never go to the woods."

"You will repent if you do," continued Tom. "But let me proceed on my journey. My bones were well-nigh dislocated before we got to D——. The roads for the last twelve miles were nothing but a succession of mud-holes, covered with the most ingenious invention ever thought of for racking the limbs, called corduroy bridges; not breeches, mind you, for I thought, whilst jolting up and down over them, that I should arrive at my destination minus that indispensable covering. It was night when we got to Mr. ——'s place. I was tired and hungry, my face disfigured and blistered by the unremitting attentions of the black flies that rose in swarms from the river. I thought to get a private room to wash and dress in, but there is no such thing as privacy in this country. In the bush, all things are in common; you cannot even get a bed without having to share it with a companion. A bed on the floor in a public sleeping-room! Think of that: a public sleeping-room! — men, women, and children, only divided by a paltry curtain. Oh, ye gods! think of the snoring, squalling, grumbling, puffing; think of the kicking, elbowing, and crowding; the suffocating heat, the mosquitoes, with their infernal buzzing — and you will form some idea of the misery I endured the first night of my arrival in the bush.

"But these are not half the evils with which you have to contend. You are pestered with nocturnal visitants far more disagreeable than even the mosquitoes, and must put up with annoyances more disgusting than the crowded close room. And then, to appease the cravings of hunger, fat pork is served to you three times a day. No wonder that the Jews eschewed the vile animal; they were people of taste. Pork, morning, noon, and night, swimming in its own grease! The bishop who complained of partridges every day should have been condemned to three months' feeding upon pork in the bush; and he would have become an anchorite, to escape the horrid sight of swine's flesh for ever spread before him. No wonder I am thin; I have been starved — starved upon fritters and pork, and that disgusting specimen of unleavened bread, yclept cakes in the pan.

"I had such a horror of the pork diet, that whenever I saw the dinner in progress I fled to the canoe, in the hope of drowning upon the waters all reminiscences of the hateful banquet; but even here the very fowls of the air and the reptiles of the deep lifted up their voices, and shouted, 'Pork, pork, pork!' "

M—— remonstrated with his friend for deserting the

country for such minor evils as these, which, after all, he said, could easily be borne.

"Easily borne!" exclaimed the indignant Wilson. "Go and try them; and then tell me that. I did try to bear them with a good grace, but it would not do. I offended everybody with my grumbling. I was constantly reminded by the ladies of the house that gentlemen should not come to this country without they were able to put up with a *little* inconvenience; that I should make as good a settler as a butterfly in a beehive; that it was impossible to be nice about food and dress in the *bush*; that people must learn to eat what they could get, and be content to be shabby and dirty, like their neighbours in the *bush*, until that horrid word *bush* became synonymous with all that was hateful and revolting in my mind.

"It was impossible to keep anything to myself. The children pulled my books to pieces to look at the pictures; and an impudent, bare-legged Irish servant girl took my towels to wipe the dishes with, and my clothes-brush to black the shoes — an operation which she performed with a mixture of soot and grease. I thought I should be better off in a place of my own, so I bought a wild farm that was recommended to me, and paid for it double what it was worth. When I came to examine my estate, I found there was no house upon it, and I should have to wait until the fall to get one put up, and a few acres cleared for cultivation. I was glad to return to my old quarters.

"Finding nothing to shoot in the woods, I determined to amuse myself with fishing; but Mr. —— could not always lend his canoe, and there was no other to be had. To pass away the time, I set about making one. I bought an axe, and went to the forest to select a tree. About a mile from the lake, I found the largest pine I ever saw. I did not much like to try my maiden hand upon it, for it was the first and the last tree I ever cut down. But to it I went; and I blessed God that it reached the ground without killing me in its way thither. When I was about it, I thought I might as well make the canoe big enough; but the bulk of the tree deceived me in the length of my vessel, and I forgot to measure the one that belonged to Mr. —— . It took me six weeks hollowing it out, and when it was finished it was as long as a sloop-of-war, and too unwieldy for all the oxen in the township to draw it to the water. After all my labour, my combats with those wood-demons the black flies, sand-flies, and mosquitoes, my boat remains a useless monument of my industry. And worse than this, the fatigue I had endured, while working at it late and early, brought on the ague; which so disgusted me with the country that I sold my farm and all my traps for an old song; purchased Bruin to bear me company on my voyage home; and the moment I am able to get rid of this tormenting fever, I am off."

Argument and remonstrance were alike in vain, he could not be dissuaded from his purpose. Tom was as obstinate as his bear.

The next morning he conducted us to the stable to see Bruin. The young denizen of the forest was tied to the manger, quietly masticating a cob of Indian corn, which he held in his paw, and looked half human as he sat upon his haunches, regarding us with a solemn, melancholy air. There was an extraordinary likeness, quite ludicrous, between Tom and the bear. We said nothing, but exchanged glances. Tom read our thoughts.

"Yes," said he, "there is a strong resemblance; I saw it when I bought him. Perhaps we are brothers;" and taking in his hand the chain that held the bear, he bestowed upon him sundry fraternal caresses, which the ungrateful Bruin returned with low and savage growls.

"He can't flatter. He's all truth and sincerity. A child of nature, and worthy to be my friend; the only Canadian I ever mean to acknowledge as such."

About an hour after this, poor Tom was shaking with ague,

which in a few days reduced him so low that I began to think he would never see his native shores again. He bore the affliction very philosophically, and all his well days he spent with us.

One day my husband was absent, having accompanied Mr. S —— to inspect a farm, which he afterwards purchased, and I had to get through the long day in the best manner I could. The local papers were soon exhausted. At that period, they possessed little or no interest for me. I was astonished and disgusted at the abusive manner in which they were written, the freedom of the press being enjoyed to an extent in this province unknown in more civilized communities.

Men, in Canada, may call one another rogues and miscreants, in the most approved Billingsgate, through the medium of the newspapers, which are a sort of safety-valve to let off all the bad feelings and malignant passions floating through the country, without any dread of the horsewhip. Hence it is the commonest thing in the world to hear one editor abusing, like a pickpocket, an opposition brother; calling him a *reptile — a crawling thing — a calumniator — a hired vendor of lies*; and his paper a *smut-machine —a vile engine of corruption, as base and degraded as the proprietor,* &c. Of this description was the paper I now held in my hand, which had the impudence to style itself the *Reformer* — not of morals or manners, certainly, if one might judge by the vulgar abuse that defiled every page of the precious document. I soon flung it from me, thinking it worthy of the fate of many a better production in the older times, that of being burned by the common hangman; but, happily, the office of hangman has become obsolete in Canada, and the editors of these refined journals may go on abusing their betters with impunity.

Books I had none, and I wished that Tom would make his appearance, and amuse me with his oddities; but he had suffered so much from the ague the day before that when he did enter the room to lead me to dinner, he looked like a walking corpse — the dead among the living! so dark, so livid, so melancholy, it was really painful to look upon him.

"I hope the ladies who frequent the ordinary won't fall in love with me," said he, grinning at himself in the miserable looking-glass that formed the case of the Yankee clock, and was ostentatiously displayed on a side table; "I look quite killing today. What a comfort it is, Mrs. M—— , to be above all rivalry."

In the middle of dinner, the company was disturbed by the entrance of a person who had the appearance of a gentleman, but who was evidently much flustered with drinking. He thrust his chair in between two gentlemen who sat near the head of the table, and in a loud voice demanded fish.

"Fish, sir?" said the obseqious waiter, a great favourite with all persons who frequented the hotel; "there is no fish, sir. There was a fine salmon, sir, had you come sooner; but 'tis all eaten, sir."

"Then fetch me something, smart!"

"I'll see what I can do, sir," said the obliging Tim, hurrying out.

Tom Wilson was at the head of the table, carving a roast pig, and was in the act of helping a lady, when the rude fellow thrust his fork into the pig, calling out as he did so —

"Hold, sir! give me some of that pig! You have eaten among you all the fish, and now you are going to appropriate the best parts of the pig."

Tom raised his eyebrows, and stared at the stranger in his peculiar manner, then very coolly placed the whole of the pig on his plate. "I have heard," he said, "of dog eating dog, but I never before saw pig eating pig."

"Sir! do you mean to insult me?" cried the stranger, his face crimsoning with anger.

"Only to tell you, sir, that you are no gentleman. Here, Tim," turning to the waiter, "go to the stable and bring in my bear; we will place him at the table to teach this man how

22

to behave himself in the presence of ladies."

A general uproar ensued; the women left the table, while the entrance of the bear threw the gentlemen present into convulsions of laughter. It was too much for the human biped; he was forced to leave the room, and succumb to the bear.

My husband concluded his purchase of the farm, and invited Wilson to go with us into the country and try if change of air would be beneficial to him; for in his then weak state it was impossible for him to return to England. His funds were getting very low, and Tom thankfully accepted the offer. Leaving Bruin in the charge of Tim (who delighted in the oddities of the strange English gentleman), Tom made one of our party to ———— .

BRÉBEUF'S LAST JOURNEY
E. J. Pratt

No doubt in the mind of Brébeuf that this was the last
Journey — three miles over the snow. He knew
That the margins as thin as they were by which he escaped
From death through the eighteen years of his mission toil
Did not belong to this chapter: not by his pen
Would this be told. He knew his place in the line,
For the blaze of the trail that was cut on the bark by Jogues
Shone still. He had heard the story as told by writ
And word of survivors — of how a captive slave
Of the hunters, the skin of his thighs cracked with the frost,
He would steal from the tents to the birches, make a rough
    cross
From two branches, set it in snow and on the peel
Inscribe his vows and dedicate to the Name
In "litanies of love" what fragments were left
From the wrack of his flesh; of his escape from the tribes;
Of his journey to France where he knocked at the door of
    the College
Of Rennes, was gathered in as a mendicant friar,
Nameless, unknown, till he gave for proof to the priest
His scarred credentials of faith, the nail-less hands
And withered arms — the signs of the Mohawk fury.
Nor yet was the story finished — he had come again
Back to his mission to get the second death.
And the comrades of Jogues — Goupil, Eustache and Couture,
Had been stripped and made to run the double files
And take the blows — one hundred clubs to each line —
And this as the prelude to torture, leisured, minute,
Where thorns on the quick, scallop shells to the joints
    of the thumbs,
Provided the sport for children and squaws till the end.
And adding salt to the blood of Brébeuf was the thought
Of Daniel — was it months or a week ago?
So far, so near, it seemed in time, so close
In leagues — just over there to the south it was
He faced the arrows and died in front of his church.

But winding into the greater artery
Of thought that bore upon the coming passion
Were little tributaries of wayward wish
And reminiscence. Paris with its vespers
Was folded in the mind of Lalemant,
And the soft Gothic lights and traceries
Were shading down the ridges of his vows.
But two years past at Bourges he had walked the cloisters,
Companioned by Saint Augustine and Francis,
And wrapped in quiet holy mists. Brébeuf,
His mind a moment throwing back the curtain
Of eighteen years, could see the orchard lands,
The *cidreries*, the peasants at the Fairs,
The undulating miles of wheat and barley,
Gardens and pastures rolling like a sea
From Lisieux to Le Havre. Just now the surf
Was pounding on the limestone Norman beaches
And on the reefs of Calvados. Had dawn
This very day not flung her surplices
Around the headlands and with golden fire
Consumed the silken argosies that made
For Rouen from the estuary of the Seine?
A moment only for that veil to lift —
A moment only for those bells to die
That rang their matins at Condé-sur-Vire.

By noon St. Ignace! The arrival there
The signal for the battle-cries of triumph,
The gauntlet of the clubs. The stakes were set
And the ordeal of Jogues was re-enacted
Upon the priests — even with wilder fury,
For here at last was trapped their greatest victim,
Echon. The Iroquois had waited long
For this event. Their hatred for the Hurons
Fused with their hatred for the French and priests
Was to be vented on this sacrifice,

And to that camp had come apostate Hurons,
United with their foes in common hate
To settle up their reckoning with *Echon.*

       .   .   .

Now three o'clock, and capping the height of the passion,
Confusing the sacraments under the pines of the forest,
Under the incense of balsam, under the smoke
Of the pitch, was offered the rite of the font. On the head,
The breast, the loins and the legs, the boiling water!
While the mocking paraphrase of the symbols was hurled
At their faces like shards of flint from the arrow heads —
"We baptize thee with water . . .
                          That thou mayest be led
To Heaven . . .
                To that end we do anoint thee.
We treat thee as a friend: we are the cause
Of thy happiness; we are thy priests; the more
Thou sufferest, the more thy God will reward thee,
So give us thanks for our kind offices."

The fury of taunt was followed by fury of blow.
Why did not the flesh of Brébeuf cringe to the scourge,
Respond to the heat, for rarely the Iroquois found
A victim that would not cry out in such pain — yet here
The fire was on the wrong fuel. Whenever he spoke,
It was to rally the soul of his friend whose turn
Was to come through the night while the eyes were uplifted
     in prayer,
Imploring the Lady of Sorrows, the mother of Christ,
As pain brimmed over the cup and the will was called
To stand the test of the coals. And sometimes the speech
Of Brébeuf struck out, thundering reproof to his foes,
Half-rebuke, half-defiance, giving them roar for roar.
Was it because the chancel became the arena,

Brébeuf a lion at bay, not a lamb on the altar,
As if the might of a Roman were joined to the cause
Of Judaea? Speech they could stop for they girdled his lips,
But never a moan could they get. Where was the source
Of his strength, the home of his courage that topped the best
Of their braves and even out-fabled the lore of their legends?
In the bunch of his shoulders which often had carried a load
Extorting the envy of guides at an Ottawa portage?
The heat of the hatchets was finding a path to that source.
In the thews of his thighs which had mastered the trails of the
    Neutrals?
They would gash and beribbon those muscles. Was it the
    blood?
They would draw it fresh from its fountain. Was it the heart?
They dug for it, fought for the scraps in the way of the wolves.
But not in these was the valour or stamina lodged;
Nor in the symbol of Richelieu's robes or the seals
Of Mazarin's charters, nor in the stir of the *lilies*
Upon the Imperial folds; nor yet in the words
Loyola wrote on a table of lava-stone
In the cave of Manresa — not in these the source —
But in the sound of invisible trumpets blowing
Around two slabs of board, right-angled, hammered
By Roman nails and hung on a Jewish hill.

THE NAMING OF ALBERT JOHNSON
Rudy Wiebe

1. *The Eagle River, Yukon: Wednesday, 17 February 1932*
Tuesday, 16 February

There is arctic silence at last, after the long snarl of rifles. As
if all the stubby trees within earshot had finished splitting in
the cold. Then the sound of the airplane almost around the
river's bend begins to return, turning as tight a spiral as it
may up over bank and trees and back down, over the man
crumpled on the bedroll, over the frantic staked dogteams,
spluttering, down, glancing down off the wind-ridged river.
Tail leaping, almost cartwheeling over its desperate roar for
skis, immense sound rocketing from that bouncing black dot
on the level glare but stopped finally, its prop whirl
staggering out motionless just behind the man moving
inevitably forward on snowshoes, not looking back, step by
step up the river with his rifle ready. Hesitates, lifts one foot,
then the other, stops, and moves forward again to the splotch
in the vast whiteness before him.

The pack is too huge, and apparently worried by rats with
very long, fine teeth. Behind it a twisted body. Unbelievably
small. One outflung hand still clutching a rifle, but no
motion, nothing, the airplane dead and only the distant
sounds of dogs somewhere, of men moving at the banks of the
river. The police rifle points down, steadily extending the
police arm until it can lever the body, already stiffening, up.
A red crater for hip. As if one small part of that incredible
toughness had rebelled at last, exploded red out of itself,
splattering itself with itself when everything but itself was at
last unreachable. But the face is turning up. Rime, and clots
of snow ground into whiskers, the fur hat hurled somewhere
by bullets perhaps, and the whipped cowlick already a mat
frozen above half-open eyes showing only white, nostrils
flared, the concrete face wiped clean of everything but snarl.
Freezing snarl and teeth. As if the long-clenched jaws had
tightened down beyond some ultimate cog and openly locked
their teeth into their own torn lips in one final wordlessly
silent scream.

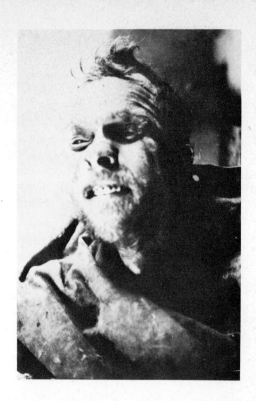

The pilot blunders up, gasping. "By god, we got the son of
a bitch!" Stumbles across the back of the snowshoes and
recovers beside the policeman. Gagging a little, "My g — "
All that sudden colour propped up by the rifle barrel on the
otherwise white snow. And the terrible face.

The one necessary bullet, in the spine where its small entry
cannot be seen at this moment, and was never felt as six others
were, knocked the man face down in the snow. Though that
would never loosen his grip on his rifle. The man had been
working himself over on his side, not concerned as it seemed
for the bullets singing to him from the level drifts in front of
him or the trees on either bank. With his left hand he was
reaching into his coat pocket to reload his Savage .30-.30,
almost warm on the inside of his other bare hand, and he
knew as every good hunter must that he had exactly
thirty-nine bullets left besides the one hidden under the rifle's
butt plate. If they moved in any closer he also had the
Winchester .22 with sixty-four bullets, and closer still there
would be the sawed-off shotgun, though he had only a few

shells left, he could not now be certain exactly how many. He had stuffed snow tight into the hole where one or perhaps even two shells had exploded in his opposite hip pocket. A man could lose his blood in a minute from a hole that size but the snow was still white and icy the instant he had to glance at it, packing it in. If they had got him there before forcing him down behind his pack in the middle of the river, he could not have moved enough to pull out of the pack straps, leave alone get behind it for protection. Bullets twitch it, whine about his tea tin like his axe handle snapping once at his legs as he ran from the eastern river bank too steep to clamber up, a very bad mistake to have to discover after spending several minutes and a hundred yards of strength running his snowshoes towards it. Not a single rock, steep and bare like polished planks. But he had gained a little on them, he saw that as he curved without stopping towards the center of the river and the line of trees beyond it. That bank is easily climbed, he knows because he climbed it that morning, but all the dogs and men so suddenly around the hairpin turn surprised him towards the nearest bank, and he sees the teams spreading to outflank him, three towards the low west bank. And two of them bending over the one army radioman he got.

Instantly the man knew it was the river that had betrayed him. He had outlegged their dogs and lost the plane time and again on glare-ice and in fog and brush and between the endless trails of caribou herds, but the sluggish loops of this river doubling back on itself have betrayed him. It is his own best move, forward and then back, circle forward and further back, backwards, so the ones following his separate tracks will suddenly confront each other in cursing bewilderment. But this river, it cannot be named the Porcupine, has out-doubled him. For the dogs leaping towards him around the bend, the roaring radioman heaving at his sled, scrabbling for his rifle, this is clearly what he saw when he climbed the tree on the far bank, one of the teams he saw then across a wide tongue of land already ahead of him, as it seemed, and he started back to get further behind them before he followed and picked them off singly in whatever tracks of his they thought they were following. These dogs and this driver rounding to face him as he walks so carefully backwards in his snowshoes on the curve of his own tracks.

Whatever this river is, spiralling back into the Yukon hills, his rifle will not betray him. Words are bellowing out of the racket of teams hurtling around the bend. His rifle speaks easily, wordlessly to the army radioman kneeling, sharpshooter position, left elbow propped on left knee. The sights glided together certain and deadly, and long before the sound had returned that one kneeling was already flung back clean as frozen wood bursting at his axe.

He has not eaten, he believes it must be two days, and the rabbit tracks are so old they give no hope for his snares. The squirrel burrow may be better. He is scraping curls from tiny spruce twigs, watching them tighten against the lard pail, watching the flames as it seems they're licking the tin blacker with their gold tongues. The fire lives with him, and he will soon examine the tinfoil of matches in his pocket, and the tinfoil bundle in his pack, and also the other two paper-wrapped packages. That must be done daily, if possible. The pack, unopened, with the .22 laced to its side is between his left shoulder and the snow hollow; the moose-hides spread under and behind him; the snowshoes stuck erect into the snow on the right, the long axe lying there and the rifle also, in its cloth cover but on the moosehide pouch. He has already worked carefully on his feet, kneading as much of the frost out of one and then the other as he can before the fire, though two toes on the left are black and the heel of the right is rubbed raw. Bad lacing when he walked backwards, and too numb for him to notice. The one toe can only be kept another day, perhaps, but he has only a gun-oily rag for his heel. Gun-oil? Spruce gum? Wait. His feet are wrapped and ready to move if necessary and he sits watching warmth curl around the pail. Leans his face down into it. Then he puts the knife away in his clothes and pulls out a tiny paper. His hard fingers unfold it carefully, he studies the crystals a moment, and then as the flames tighten the blackened spirals of spruce he pours that into the steaming pail. He studies the paper, the brownness of it; the suggestion of a word beginning, or perhaps ending, that shines through its substance. He lowers it steadily then until it darkens, smiling as a spot of deep brown breaks through the possible name and curls back a black empty circle towards his fingers. He lets it go, feeling warmth like a massage in its final flare and dying. There is nothing left but a smaller fold of pepper and a bag of salt so when he drinks, it is very slowly, letting each mouthful move for every part of his tongue to hold a moment this last faint sweetness.

He sits in the small yellow globe created by fire. Drinking. The wind breathes through the small spruce, his body rests motionlessly; knowing that dug into the snow with drifts and spruce tips above him they could see his smokeless fire only if they flew directly over him. And the plane cannot fly at night. They are somewhere very close now, and their plane less than a few minutes behind. It has flown straight in an hour, again and again, all he had overlaid with tangled tracks in five weeks, but the silent land is what it is. He is now resting motionlessly. And waiting.

And the whiskey jacks are suddenly there. He had not known them before to come after dark, but grey and white tipped with black they fluffed themselves at the grey edge of his light, watching, and then one hopped two hops. Sideways. The first living thing he had seen since the caribou. But he reaches for the bits of babiche he had cut and rubbed in salt, laid ready on the cloth of the riflebutt. He throws, the draggle-tail is gone but the other watches, head cocked, then jumps so easily the long space his stiff throw had managed, and the bit is gone. He does not move his body, tosses another bit, and another, closer, closer, and then draggle-tail is there scrabbling for the bit, and he twitches the white string lying beside the bits of babiche left by the rifle, sees the bigger piece tug from the snow and draggle-tail leap to it. Gulp. He tugs, feels the slight weight as the thread lifts from the snow in the firelight, and now the other is gone while draggle-tail comes towards him inevitably, string pulling the beak soundlessly agape, wings desperate in snow, dragged between rifle and fire into the waiting claw of his hand. He felt the bird's blood beat against his palm, the legs and tail and wings thud an instant, shuddering and then limp between his relentless fingers.

Wings. Noiselessly he felt the beautiful muscles shift, slip over bones delicate as twigs. He could lope circles around any dogs they set on his trail but that beast labelled in letters combing the clouds, staring everywhere until its roar suddenly blundered up out of a canyon or over a ridge, laying its relentless shadow like words on the world: he would have dragged every tree in the Yukon together to build a fire and boil that. Steel pipes and canvas and wires and name, that stinking noise. In the silence under the spruce he skims the tiny fat bubbles from the darkening soup; watches them coagulate yellow on the shavings. Better than gun-oil, or gum. He began to unwrap his feet again but listening, always listening. The small furrow of the bird pointed towards him in the snow.

2. *The Richardson Mountains, NWT: Tuesday, 9 February 1932*
Saturday, 30 January

Though it means moving two and three miles to their one, the best trail to confuse them in the foothill ravines was a spiral zig-zag. West of the mountains he has not seen them; he has outrun them so far in crossing the Richardson Mountains during the blizzard that when he reaches a river he thought it must be the Porcupine because he seems at last to be inside something that is completely alone. But the creeks draining east lay in seemingly parallel but eventually converging canyons with tundra plateaus glazed under wind between them, and when he paused on one leg of his zag he sometimes saw them, across one plateau or in a canyon, labouring with their dogs and sleds as it seems ahead of him. In the white scream of the mountain pass where no human being has ever ventured in winter he does not dare pause to sleep for two days and the long night between them, one toe and perhaps another frozen beyond saving and parts of his face dead, but in the east he had seen the trackers up close, once been above them and watched them coming along his trails towards each other unawares out of two converging canyons with their sleds and drivers trailing, and suddenly round the cliff to face each other in cursing amazement. He was far enough not to hear their words as they heated water for tea, wasting daylight minutes, beating their hands to keep warm.

The police drive the dog teams now, and the Indians sometimes; the ones who can track him on the glazed snow, through zags and bends, always wary of ambush, are the two army radiomen. One of the sleds is loaded with batteries when it should be food, but they sniff silently along his tracks, loping giant circles ahead of the heaving dogs and swinging arms like semaphores when they find a trail leading as it seems directly back towards the sleds they have just left. He would not have thought them so relentless at unravelling his trails, these two who every morning tried to raise the police on their frozen radio, and when he was convinced they would follow him as certainly as Millen and the plane roared up, dropping supplies, it was time to accept the rising blizzard over the mountains and find at last, for certain, the Porcupine River.

It is certainly Millen who brought the plane north just before the blizzard, and it was Millen who saw his smoke and heard him coughing, whistling in that canyon camp hidden in trees under a cliff so steep he has to chop handholds in the frozen rock to get out of there. Without dynamite again, or bombs, they could not dig him out; even in his unending alert his heart jerks at the sound of what was a foot slipping against a frozen tree up the ridge facing him. His rifle is out of its

sheath, the shell racking home in the cold like precise steel
biting. There is nothing more; an animal? A tree bursting? He
crouches motionless, for if they are there they should be all
around him, perhaps above on the cliff, and he will not move
until he knows. Only the wind worrying spruce and snow,
whining wordlessly. There, twenty yards away a shadow
moves, Millen certainly, and his shot snaps as his rifle swings
up, as he drops. Bullets snick from everywhere, their sound
booming back and forth along the canyon. He has only fired
once and is down, completely aware, on the wrong side of his
fire and he shoots carefully again to draw their shots and they
come, four harmlessly high and nicely spaced out: there are
two — Millen and another — below him in the canyon and
two a bit higher on the right ridge, one of them that slipped.
Nothing up the canyon or above on the cliff. With that
knowledge he gathered himself and leaped over the fire against
the cliff and one on the ridge made a good shot that cut his
jacket and he could fall as if gut-shot in the hollow of
deadfall. Until the fire died, he was almost comfortable.

In the growing dusk he watches the big Swede, who drove
dogs very well, crawl towards Millen stretched out, face down.
He watches him tie Millen's legs together with the laces of his
mukluks and drag him backwards, plowing a long furrow and
leaving the rifle sunk in the snow. He wastes no shot at their
steady firing, and when they stop there are Millen's words still
    You're surrounded. King isn't dead. Will you
   give
waiting, frozen in the canyon. He lay absolutely motionless
behind the deadfall against the cliff, as if he were dead,
knowing they would have to move finally. He flexed his feet
continuously, and his fingers as he shifted the rifle no more
quickly than a clock hand, moving into the position it would
have to be when they charged him. They almost out-wait him;
it is really a question between the coming darkness and his
freezing despite his invisible motions, but before darkness
Millen had to move. Two of them were coming and he shifted

his rifle slightly on the log to cover the left one — it must have been the long cold that made him mistake that for Millen — who dived out of sight, his shot thundering along the canyon, but Millen did not drop behind anything. Simply down on one knee, firing. Once, twice, bullets tore the log and then he had his head up with those eyes staring straight down his sights and he fired two shots so fast the roar in the canyon sounded as one and Millen stood up, the whole length over him, whirled in that silent unmistakable way, and crashed face down in the snow. He hears them dragging and chopping trees for a stage cache to keep the body, and in the darkness he chops handholds up the face of the cliff, step by step, as he hoists himself and his pack out of another good shelter. As he has had to leave others.

3. *The Rat River, NWT: Saturday, 10 January 1932*
Thursday, 31 December 1931
Tuesday, 28 July

In his regular round of each loophole he peers down the promontory towards their fires glaring up from behind the river bank. They surround him on three sides, nine of them with no more than forty dogs, which in this cold means they already need more supplies than they can have brought with them. They will be making plans for something, suddenly, beyond bullets against his logs and guns and it will have to come soon. In the long darkness, and he can wait far easier than they. Dynamite. If they have any more to thaw out very carefully after blowing open the roof and stovepipe as darkness settled, a hole hardly big enough for one of them — a Norwegian, they were everywhere with their long noses — to fill it an instant, staring down at him gathering himself from the corner out of roof-sod and pipes and snow: the cabin barely stuck above the drifts but that one was gigantic to lean in like that, staring until he lifted his rifle and the long face vanished an instant before his bullet passed through that space. But the hole was large enough for the cold to slide down along the wall and work itself into his trench, which would be all that saved him when they used the last of their dynamite. He began to feel what they had stalked him with all day: cold tightening steadily as steel around toes, face, around fingers.

In the clearing still nothing stirs. There is only the penumbra of light along the circle of the bank as if they had laid a trench-fire to thaw the entire promontory and were soundlessly burrowing in under him. Against the earth, his face momentarily knows them coming, there. Their flares were long dead, the sky across the river flickering with orange lights to vanish down into spruce and willows again, like the shadow blotting a notch in the eastern bank, and he thrust his rifle through the chink and had almost got a shot away when a projectile arched against the sky and he jerked the gun out, diving, into the trench deep under the wall among the moose-hides that could not protect him from the roof and walls tearing apart so loud it seemed most of himself had been blasted to the farthest granules of sweet, silent, earth. The sods and foot-thick logs he had built together where the river curled were gone and he would climb out and walk away as he always had, but first he pulled himself up and out between the splinters, still holding the rifle, just in time to see yellow light humpling through the snow towards him and he fired three times so fast it sounded in his ears as though his cabin was continuing to explode. The shadows around the light dance in one spot an instant but come on in a straight black line, lengthening down, faster, and the light cuts straight across his eyes and he gets away the fourth shot and the light tears itself into bits. He might have been lying on his back staring up into night and had the stars explode into existence above him. And whatever darkness is left before him then blunders away, desperately plowing away from him through the snow like the first one who came twice with a voice repeating at his door

I am Constable Alfred King, are you in there?
fist thudding the door the second time with a paper creaking

37

louder than his voice so thin in the cold silence

    I have a search warrant now, we have had
    complaints and if you don't open

and then plowing away in a long desperate scrabble through
the sun-shot snow while the three others at the river bank
thumped their bullets hopelessly high into the logs but
shattering the window again and again until they dragged
King and each other headfirst over the edge while he placed
lead carefully over them, snapping willow bits on top of them
and still seeing, strangely, the tiny hole that had materialized
up into his door when he flexed the trigger, still hearing the
grunt that had wormed in through the slivers of the board he
had whipsawn himself. Legs and feet wrapped in moose-hide
lay a moment across his window, level in the snow, jerking as
if barely attached to a body knocked over helpless, a face
somewhere twisted in gradually developing pain that had first
leaned against his door, fist banging while that other one held
the dogs at the edge of the clearing, waiting

    Hallo? Hallo? This is Constable Alfred King of
    the Royal Canadian Mounted Police. I want to
    talk to you. Constable Millen has

and they looked into each other's eyes, once, through his tiny
window. The eyes peering down into his — could he be seen
from out of the blinding sun? — squinted blue from a boy's
round face with a bulging nose bridged over pale with cold.
King, of the Royal Mounted. Like a silly book title, or the
funny papers. He didn't look it as much as Spike Millen, main
snooper and tracker at Arctic Red River, who baked pies and
danced, everybody said, better than any man in the north. Let
them dance hipped in snow, get themselves dragged away
under spruce and dangling traps, asking, laying words on
him, naming things

    You come across from the Yukon? You got a
    trapper's licence? The Loucheaux trap the Rat,
    up towards the Richardson Mountains. You'll
    need a licence, why not

38

Words. Dropping out of nothing into advice. Maybe he wanted a kicker to move that new canoe against the Rat River? Loaded down as it is. The Rat drops fast, you have to hand-line the portage anyway to get past Destruction City where those would-be Klondikers wintered in '98. He looked up at the trader above him on the wedge of gravel. He had expected at least silence. From a trader standing with the bulge of seven hundred dollars in his pocket; in the south a man could feed himself with that for two years. Mouths always full of words, pushing, every mouth falling open and dropping words from nothing into meaning. The trader's eyes shifted finally, perhaps to the junction of the rivers behind them, south and west, the united river clicking under the canoe. As he raised his paddle. The new rifle oiled and ready with its butt almost touching his knees as he kneels, ready to pull the canoe around.

4. *Above Fort McPherson, NWT: Tuesday, 7 July 1931*

The Porcupine River, as he thought it was then, chuckled between the three logs of his raft. He could hear that below him, under the mosquitoes probing the mesh about his head, and see the gold lengthen up the river like the canoe that would come towards him from the north where the sun just refused to open the spiky horizon. Gilded, hammered out slowly, soundlessly towards him the thick gold. He sat almost without breathing, watching it come like silence. And then imperceptibly the black spired river-bend grew pointed, stretched itself in a thin straight line double-bumped, gradually spreading a straight wedge below the sun through the golden river. When he had gathered that slowly into anger it was already too late to choke his fire; the vee had abruptly bent towards him, the bow man already raised his paddle; hailed. Almost it seemed as if a name had been blundered into the silence, but he did not move in his fury. The river chuckled again.

" . . . o-o-o-o . . . " the point of the wedge almost under

him now. And the sound of a name, that was so clear he could almost distinguish it. Perhaps he already knew what it was, had long since lived this in that endlessly enraged chamber of himself, even to the strange Indian accent mounded below him in the canoe bow where the black hump of the stern partner moved them straight towards him out of the fanned ripples, crumpling gold. To the humps of his raft below on the gravel waiting to anchor them.

"What d'ya want?"

"You Albert Johnson?"

It could have been the stern man who named him. The sun like hatchet-strokes across slanted eyes, the gaunt noses below him there holding the canoe against the current, their paddles hooked in the logs of his raft. Two Loucheaux half-faces, black and red, kneeling in the roiled gold of the river, the words thudding softly in his ears.

You Albert Johnson?

One midnight above the Arctic Circle to hear again the inevitability of name. He has not heard it in four years, it could be to the very day since that Vancouver garden, staring into the evening sun and hear this quiet sound from these motionless — perhaps they are men kneeling there, perhaps waiting for him to accept again what has now been laid inevitably upon him, the name come to meet him in his journey north, come out of north around the bend and against the current of the Peel River, as they name that too, to confront him on a river he thought another and aloud where he would have found after all his years, at long last, only nameless silence.

You Albert Johnson?

"Yes," he said finally.

And out of his rage he begins to gather words together. Slowly, every word he can locate, as heavily as he would gather stones on a Saskatchewan field, to hold them for one violent moment against himself between his two hands before he heaves them up and hurls them — but they are gone. The ripples of their passing may have been smoothing out as he stares at where they should have been had they been there. Only the briefly golden river lies before him, whatever its name may be since it must have one, bending back somewhere beyond that land, curling back upon itself in its giant, relentless spirals down to the implacable, and ice-choked, arctic sea.

THE LAW OF THE YUKON
Robert W. Service

This is the law of the Yukon, and ever she makes it plain:
"Send not your foolish and feeble; send me your strong and
　　your sane.
Strong for the red rage of battle; sane, for I harry them sore;
Send me men girt for the combat, men who are grit to the
　　core;
Swift as the panther in triumph, fierce as the bear in defeat,
Sired of a bulldog parent, steeled in the furnace heat.
Send me the best of your breeding, lend me your chosen ones;
Them will I take to my bosom, them will I call my sons;
Them will I gild with my treasure, them will I glut with my
　　meat;
But the others — the misfits, the failures — I trample under
　　my feet.
Dissolute, damned, and despairful, crippled and palsied and
　　slain,
Ye would send me the spawn of your gutters — Go! take back
　　your spawn again."

"Wild and wide are my borders, stern as death is my sway;
From my ruthless throne I have ruled alone for a million years
　　and a day;
Hugging my mighty treasure, waiting for man to come:
Till he swept like a turbid torrent, and after him swept — the
　　scum.
The pallid pimp of the dead-line, the enervate of the pen,
One by one I weeded them out, for all that I sought was —
　　Men.
One by one I dismayed them, frighting them sore with my
　　glooms;
One by one I betrayed them unto my manifold dooms.
Drowned them like rats in my rivers, starved them like curs
　　on my plains,
Rotted the flesh that was left them, poisoned the blood in
　　their veins;

42

Burst with my winter upon them, searing forever their sight,
Lashed them with fungus-white faces, whimpering wild in the
    night;
Staggering blind through the storm-whirl, stumbling mad
    through the snow,
Frozen stiff in the ice pack, brittle and bent like a bow;
Featureless, formless, forsaken, scented by wolves in their
    flight,
Left for the wind to make music through ribs that are
    glittering white;
Gnawing the black crust of failure, searching the pit of
    despair,
Crooking the toe in the trigger, trying to patter a prayer;
Going outside with an escort, raving with lips all afoam;
Writing a cheque for a million, drivelling feebly of home;
Lost like a louse in the burning . . . or else in tented town
Seeking a drunkard's solace, sinking and sinking down;
Steeped in the slime at the bottom, dead to a decent world,
Lost 'mid the human flotsam, far on the frontier hurled;
In the camp at the bend of the river, with its dozen saloons
    aglare,
Its gambling dens a-riot, its gramophones all a-blare;
Crimped with the crimes of a city, sin-ridden and bridled with
    lies,
In the hush of my mountained vastness, in the flush of my
    midnight skies.
Plague-spots, yet tools of my purpose, so natheless I suffer
    them thrive,
Crushing my Weak in their clutches, that only my Strong
    may survive."

"But the others, the men of my mettle, the men who would
    'stablish my fame,
Unto its ultimate issue, winning me honour, not shame;
Searching my uttermost valleys, fighting each step as they go,

Shooting the wrath of my rapids, scaling my ramparts of
    snow;
Ripping the guts of my mountains, looting the beds of my
    creeks,
Them will I take to my bosom, and speak as a mother speaks.
I am the land that listens, I am the land that broods;
Steeped in eternal beauty, crystalline waters and woods.
Long have I waited lonely, shunned as a thing accurst,
Monstrous, moody, pathetic, the last of the lands and the
    first;

Visioning camp-fires at twilight, sad with a longing forlorn,
Feeling my womb o'er-pregnant with the seed of cities
        unborn.
Wild and wide are my borders, stern as death is my sway,
And I wait for the men who will win me — and I will not be
        won in a day;
And I will not be won by weaklings, subtile, suave, and mild,
But by men with the hearts of vikings, and the simple faith of
        a child;
Desperate, strong, and resistless, unthrottled by fear or defeat,
Them will I gild with my treasure, them will I glut with my
        meat."

"Lofty I stand from each sister land, patient and wearily wise,
With the weight of a world of sadness in my quiet, passionless
        eyes;
Dreaming alone of a people, dreaming alone of a day,
When men shall not rape my riches, and curse me and go
        away;
Making a bawd of my bounty, fouling the hand that gave —
Till I rise in my wrath and I sweep on their path and I stamp
        them into a grave.
Dreaming of men who will bless me, of women esteeming me
        good,
Of children born in my borders, of radiant motherhood;
Of cities leaping to stature, of fame like a flag unfurled,
As I pour the tide of my riches in the eager lap of the world."

This is the Law of the Yukon, that only the Strong shall
        thrive;
That surely the Weak shall perish, and only the Fit survive.
Dissolute, damned, and despairful, crippled and palsied and
        slain,
This is the Will of the Yukon — Lo! how she makes it plain.

THE MOVIES COME TO GULL POINT
Will R. Bird

Four men were mending nets in a shack behind the fish wharf at Granny's Cove. Spring had come grudgingly, but now the warm sun was melting the ice and sending steamy vapours from tarred roofs. The Cove front murmured with activity as all its men prepared for the sea.

The four worked in silence, seated on benches, half-hidden by the drab folds that hung from the cross-beams overhead, their hands flicking in and out among the meshes, tying, knotting, threading. All at once they paused and listened. There were new voices outside.

"Them's the two back from pulp-cuttin'," said Simon Holder. He was a small lean man.

"Wonder if they got their pay," said Dick Berry, a red-faced man with big bony shoulders.

The two working in the rear were young, and brothers, Ben and Matthew Crowdy, proud of being hired with Simon. Ben was only seventeen, and slim, but he carried himself as seriously as the other three.

"Ho, Willyum," shouted Berry as a man passed the open door. "Don't rush yourself. What's the word down along?"

The man came back and peered in at them. "Not much new," he said. "They're havin' movin' pictures . . . "

"Movin'!" Berry's mouth fell open. "How?"

"The man's got a machine'n engine to drive her. He's over't Gull Point tonight givin' a showin'."

"Over't Gull Point!" Berry rose from his bench, his red face glowing. "Simon, let's go over?"

"What's he chargin'?" asked Simon.

"Twenty-five cents, but he's got good pictures. There's one . . ."

"Don't tell us," blurted Matthew. "That would spoil it. What say we go, Simon?" He had a solemn face, like Ben, but his eyes were bright.

Simon left his bench and went outside. The others followed him and they stood, gazing at the sea.

The ice was breaking up. The warm sun had been aided by a strong wind off land and a lane of black water was steadily widening along the foot of the cliffs, while smaller leads angled in all directions, opening as the pack surged and loosened. Southward, toward Gull Point, there seemed plenty of open sea.

"Risky," pronounced Simon.

"Chancy," agreed Berry, "but not too much."

"Wind's favourin' too," added Matthew.

There was a slow shrill screaming of the ice. Floes and pans were grinding together; the harsh noises never stilled.

Ben looked up. There were no clouds and the sky was a blue that seemed to reflect the endless ice.

"Looks fairish weather," he said, "but it's comin' tonight."

"You boys got money?" asked Simon.

They shook their heads and Berry grinned.

"That makes a dollar," Simon said gravely. "That's a lot of money."

"There ain't never been," said Ben, "movin' pictures up here. I never seen any in my life."

"Bet she's open to the Point," said Berry. "We'd do fine with a lugsail."

Simon rubbed his salt-bitten chin. They four were the best in the Cove. "Git geared," he said suddenly.

"It's six mile," Simon said an hour later. They had launched their dory and were well into the wide lead but the lugsail was proving a menace. A stiffer breeze caught them and tipped the boat. He pulled the canvas in. "Mebbe we're fools."

They had lost much time. Matthew had broken a thole pin in his eagerness and they had not turned back to repair it. They had trusted in the sail, and his oars were idle.

"The wind'll be strong outside," said Berry. He was rowing and he grunted his words.

They were true enough. Once away from the shelter of the high black cliffs, the wind caught the dory and they swung along sharply. There were many wide lanes and the sea was running higher than it had seemed, and spray flung over them.

Simon steered with a long sweep and Matthew was seated next him, squatted low but ready to lend a hand. As they swayed with the dory all four seemed a jumble of sou'westers and oilskins.

They did not attempt conversation. The shrieking, jarring crashes of the ice mingled with the whistling of the breeze and drowned all lesser sounds. The rapidly widening lane they were in became a sea of racing, tumbling water that spewed spray as it struck the dory. Simon's oilskins dripped and his cheeks were wet but his expression never changed. He was gauging every wave with the instinct of one born to the sea.

Suddenly each man braced himself for action. A loose floe hove in their path and the waves pitched it about dangerously. Simon and Berry used all their strength and skill as they managed to avoid it, but neither man spoke. Matthew was bailing instantly and they moved slowly until he had scooped from the dory the gallons of water shipped during the swinging manoeuvre. It seemed, in that short time, to become night.

The rocky point behind them had cut off the sun as it sank rapidly, and with its going the wind keened to a penetrating chill. The darkness added greatly to their risks and Matthew peered ahead.

"She's started to fog," he shouted. "She's a bank now."

The shore, hazy before, had become mist-drowned, shrouded with a thick white creeping veil. It seemed to permeate the air.

"She's come behind the same," yelled Ben.

They were half their journey and a swirling blanket of gray vapours closed about them. They would have to chance their passage ahead where the contour of the coast veered so that the slow-moving field of ice might bar their way.

It was Matthew who first saw that they had entered a wide

48

lane and were between shifting ice. He peered again.

"Keep straight on!" he cried.

Short waves were deluging the boat with freezing spray. Berry rowed with quick strokes, and the roar of wind and grinding ice filled the night.

The water became smoother. Matthew reached and touched Berry on the back and at the signal the bigger man changed places with him. They were tense and watchful; only men of their experience could know the risk of a channel between rafted ice. Deep booming sounds seemed to pass over them as though they had sunk in a trough of the sea, and it grew darker.

"Look!" yelled Ben. "She's closin' in."

There was a muttered undertone beneath the booming and their lane of open water had narrowed to feet in width.

They slipped awkwardly in their sealskin boots as each man scrambled onto the floe, but they secured footing and with desperate hurried strength dragged the heavy dory from the water. It taxed them to their utmost and no one spoke. The ice was an uneven surging field and a blurred grayness covered everything.

"She's bad," said Berry. "We should have . . . "

He did not finish. There was a crash of giant floes colliding and they were sprawled beside the dory. In an instant the night was a wilder chaos of wind and clamour.

"Watch out!" Simon's voice rose above the tumult like a cracking whip. "She's breakin'."

The floe buckled. It rose and lowered under them. There were sudden surgings that pitched them about. They seized the dory sides and pushed landward. The roaring of surf at the face of the floe came clearly.

"Watch her!" It was a scream more than a shout. The ice was parting.

The floe rocked and settled. Water sloshed over the ice, reached them. There was another settling.

"There!" yelled Ben.

The field had opened and the sea drove into the vent with foaming fury. It poured over the ice to meet them. Then, its weight, and the driving surf, heaved the floe.

They slid backward in the wash. Ben, caught by the dory, fell, and water washed over him. He rose, sobbing with his immersion, clinging to the dory, and, as if a signal were given, they rushed the boat toward the open water. The lane had widened into a broad lead.

Again the floe surged, and the dory slid into the water. Ben leaped into it, tilting it dangerously. Matthew sprang in beside him, rocking it to a safer keel. Berry had given a great thrust forward to clear them from the ice and as he sprang he lunged against Simon, knocking him backward.

For a heartbeat it seemed they must capsize. The churning water had caught them as the dory took its plunge. Berry grasped his oars and threw his weight against the surge. Behind them, in the screaming murk, Simon was lost to view.

Ben had seized Simon's sweep and they toiled to bring the dory about. The lane was a smother of surf. Danger hovered over every move and the water boiled with changing currents.

They drove back alongside, catching, with perfect co-ordination, a minute lull at the ice edge, and Simon, gauging their move, joined them. It was a risky plunge, challenging all their chances, but once more Berry's strength saved the dory and then they had swung away and Ben was bailing.

In the thick darkness the surf seemed wilder than before but the worst was soon behind them. Then, just ahead, a pin-point of light shone steadily.

Within ten minutes they were in calmer waters, and lamp glows began to pierce the gloom. They landed and hurried Ben, shaking and almost numbed with cold, to the nearest house.

"Us is from Granny's Cove," announced Simon. "Ben were wet on the ice. Could us dry him here?"

"Sure, the stove's red-hot." A woman wrapped in a thick

jacket and ready to leave for the hall where the movies were to be shown, answered them. "I'll git a rig for him to put on and his'll dry while we're gone."

Ben was shaking as with ague and tiny pools formed on the floor beside him as the warmth of the stove softened his frozen clothing. He drank a scalding mixture the woman provided and his trembling ceased. He stripped his sodden clothing and Matthew ranged it on a chair-back alongside the stove. Then Ben dressed in a makeshift outfit and they followed the path the woman had taken.

The building where the movies were being shown was packed with people. It was a low-roofed structure and heated by a huge box stove. There were high odours of perspiration and many faces were beaded with moisture. Children were sandwiched among their elders and every seat was taken. Simon led the way along one wall and they stood against it, tightly wedged by others who crowded after. Ben struggled from the borrowed reefer that blanketed him.

"We're lucky," he gasped, "she's jist startin'."

There were gasps and murmurings as the lamps were extinguished and the hum of a motor began. Headings appeared on the screen and a dozen voices tried to read them.

"Let teacher read 'em," bellowed a husky voice at the rear.

"'She Knew She Was Wrong'," a high-pitched voice shrilled in the darkness as "teacher" assumed her task. "Pretty Virginia . . ."

The audience had stilled. It was seeing the incredible . . . mirrored eating places . . . ladies with bare backs and cigarettes . . . bewildering dances . . . racing cars . . . a bathing beach teeming with thousands. And one face dominated.

"See that one!" said Berry hoarsely. "Her's . . . "

"Keep shut," ordered Simon in a sibilant whisper.

They watched the heroine driving in city traffic and there were cries of admiration.

"Ho!" shouted Berry. "Look at she." He clapped his hands.

"She's won'erful sharp in steerin'," responded Simon, "but . . . " He couldn't express himself.

"Her smokes," objected Ben.

Another picture began and all voices stilled. It was a story of rival airmen, and the planes in action did marvellous stunting. A flight of machines gave a thrilling performance, all manner of stunt flying.

Berry tensed, his big hands gripping a seat back. Simon breathed with sharp little intakes. Ben and Matthew gave shrill exclamations, unable to restrain themselves.

"They're hittin'!"

"No — yes — there!"

"Lookit — lookit — *lookit!*"

A dozen voices yelled with him. The airmen were shooting earthward at dizzy speed, headed toward each other.

There was a dull grinding sound and the screen went blank.

A lamp was lighted and the operator of the movie machine worked desperately with various tools. Then he came forward.

"Sorry, folks," he said, "but the machine's broke and I've got to send the piece away. I can't show any more."

There were sighs of disappointment but no one gave criticism. They began filing from the building and the night was filled with excited voices.

Ben went to change his clothes again and the woman insisted on them stopping to drink scalding tea and to eat slices of hard bread.

"Stay the night," she urged. "I've blankets enough to fix you up on the kitchen floor."

"No," refused Simon. "The fog's cleared and she's light as day. We've got a mortal sight of work to do, gettin' ready to fish."

Berry ate and drank hugely but said nothing. The unexpected ending of the show had given him vast disappointment.

It was breaking day as the dory swung to the wharf at

Granny's Cove. The sea had been much rougher than they anticipated and they had been forced to keep near the shore line all the way. For hours there had been but the creak of boat timbers and the slap of heavy water; each was silent and dull-minded.

A slight breeze stirred the morning. It was from the west and warm. There would be a perfect day. The sunrise began in a fire of orange and crimson that merged into soft pinks and changing blues. The heavens were a mass of colour.

The light spread over the hills and reached the sleeping houses. It found iced places in the hollows and they glittered like jewels.

They dragged the dory to its landing and stood away from it. Ben was bruised and stiff. Matthew had lost a mitten and each was conscious of clothing damp with spray.

"We're back," said Simon tersely, "but it were worth it."

"Sure," agreed Berry, yawning mightily. "That girl were a prime one."

"It must be great," said Matthew, "to live where you kin see won'erful sights all the time."

The light strengthened and the sea was blue as sapphire where the sun rays reached it slantingly. Still they stood, as if each were labouring with thoughts they could not put into words. Then Simon spat and faced them.

"I don't know what youse think," he said, "but takin' all them risks to make a picture don't seem right to me."

Matthew nodded gravely. "Us been thinkin' just that," he said. "It's for nothin' but pleasurin' and it's queer they ain't laws to stop it."

"Sure," added Ben, "there should be a law ag'in it. They might have been killed."

There was no further comment. Smoke began to curl from a chimney. Ben yawned again. They had expressed that which stirred them most, so they turned and filed soberly to their homes.

CANOE-TRIP
Douglas LePan

What of this fabulous country
Now that we have it reduced to a few hot hours
And sun-burn on our backs?
On this south side the countless archipelagos,
The slipway where titans sent splashing the last great
    glaciers;
And then up to the foot of the blue pole star
A wilderness,
The pinelands whose limits seem distant as Thule,
The millions of lakes once cached and forgotten,
The clearings enamelled with blueberries, rank silence about
    them;
And skies that roll all day with cloud-chimeras
To baffle the eye with portents and unwritten myths,
The flames of sunset, the lions of gold and gules.
Into this reservoir we dipped and pulled out lakes and rivers,
We strung them together and made our circuit.
Now what shall be our word as we return,
What word of this curious country?

It is good,
It is a good stock to own though it seldom pays dividends.
There are holes here and there for a gold-mine or a
    hydro-plant.
But the tartan of river and rock spreads undisturbed,
The plaid of a land with little desire to buy or sell.
The dawning light skirls out its independence;
At noon the brazen trumpets slash the air;
Night falls, the gulls scream sharp defiance;
Let whoever comes to tame this land, beware!
Can you put a bit to the lunging wind?
Can you hold wild horses by the hair?
Then have no hope to harness the energy here,
It gallops along the wind away.
But here are crooked nerves made straight,
The fracture cured no doctor could correct.

The hand and mind, reknit, stand whole for work;
The fable proves no cul-de-sac.
Now from the maze we circle back;
The map suggested a wealth of cloudy escapes;
That was a dream, we have converted the dream to act.
And what we now expect is not simplicity,
No steady breeze, or any surprise,
Orchids along the portage, white water, crimson leaves.
Content, we face again the complex task.

And yet the marvels we have seen remain.
We think of the eagles, of the fawns at the river bend,
The storms, the sudden sun, the clouds sheered downwards.
O so to move! With such immaculate decision!
O proudly as waterfalls curling like cumulus!

RIVER TWO BLIND JACKS
Dave Godfrey

This is one of my grandfather's, and like all of his, I am not
sure if it is true or not. He was an old man when I knew him;
truth and fancy ran like two tributaries from the river of his
memory. This tale was about Albert Godspeed and Reginald
Couteau, two men whom he said he knew, and the manner of
their death — which he never claimed to know but hinted at.

Yet I would never say he lied, even though he told me
many times of the bloody day he finally captured Henri La
Mort on Great Bear Lake after more than two years of trailing
— whereas my father has let me know that the closest the old
man ever came to the good side of the Mounties was when he
trained a pack of Samoyeds they had brought over from
Russia.

I am even reluctant to say he exaggerated, although he told
me many times of the wolfish days he spent with the canoe
trains bringing furs down the Great Lakes to Montreal and I
know he was not old enough to have done that unless they
hired twelve-year-old *voyageurs* in the last years before the train
drove the canoes back into the wilderness.

I call him instead a trader of truths. He lived with the men
who did all these things and more. They would not have
minded lending him a few of their great days, they who
borrowed so many of his in their own old, darkening fireside
nights.

There was a difference though in this tale of the two
one-eyed jacks, something not quite handleable at first, but a
difference that kept this one apart from all the other tales he
told of *voyageurs* and buffalo hunters and *coureurs de bois*. For he
always told it exactly the same, word after word, as though it
would be a deep pagan sacrilege, like burning a totem, to
change this tale as he so freely changed all the others.

And the place he told it then was always the same. Behind
our house, down by the sea and away from the roar of the
freeway, was an old boathouse. In the early winter nights he
would round up all the children he could find and turn them
into that decayed building where he squatted in front of a

driftwood fire and spoke sooted black mystery at the circle of scrubbed faces which surrounded him, all staring, childlike but without disdain, at his wrinkled face and peculiar costume.

He wore then, and was buried in, just as he demanded, a pair of beaded Blackfoot moccasins, navy-blue Mountie breeches so worn and holey that they barely hid the dirty grey of his longjohns, a Cree deer-hide jacket over a flannel shirt, and, surmounting all, the black English bowler which he claimed was a present from Queen Victoria.

Here then are the words of his tale, as closely as I can remember them, but you will have to make for yourself the dry sea odour of burning driftwood and the old image of the grandfather in his black bowler with the greys of his eyes shimmering as he reached into the burnt-over timber of his past for the unblackened log of his first-son tale and totem.

For a long time, before the Klondike days, there was a feud and a battle between them two logging camps which used to squat up on the two sides of the Minassi. No one of us ever knew just exactly how it all began — we figured probably just a little friendly log-rolling contest which rolled on until it was a holy war.

One camp was Frenchies and the other weren't, which may have had something to do with it, but like all wars it was over something cockeyed and hogo'd, and it had its own rules and decorations like a Blackfoot's war tepee or a Frenchie's way of duelling. Each fall both camps picked out their champion. Then these two went up into the wilderness to fight for eight days. The camp that claimed the winning champion got to use the Minassi first after break-up.

Now before they learned how to stamp logs this may have been worth something, since the first camp out to sea always got higher prices for their timber, but now it was as useless as my breeches. They prove I once was a Mountie, but then too they keep me from wearing something that might leave me a little warmer in the winter. Stupidity's hard to kill as a turtle. Them one-eyed jacks never knew how hogo that war was making them. I could smell them all the way from Double Mont.

Double Mont was the town that served the two camps and a few others like them. It had been laid out by the same turtle brain that set up the camps, split right in half like a snake's tongue. One side for Frenchies, the other side for that unchristian mongrel of folk what made up the other camp — some Dutch, a few Germans, the odd Yankee who had broken away from the apron string of his stars and eagles, but mostly English, and mostly the second-son kind of English, don't matter if they was sons of butchers or barons, the cockeyed, hogo'd kind like Albert Godspeed, all ready to open up his dartboard and fight the Dutchies or the Chinks or the Yankees, and the ones he liked to fight the most was the ones like Reginald Couteau who could call Albert Godspeed a newcomer and a ladyfoot, because their grandfathers had been born here, in this land, and not in some hogo country on the wrong side of the ocean like newcomer Albert Godspeed. Reginald dug in under his hide one night in town.

"Not only was born his *grandpère* in dat country hogo, and also his *père,* but he himself. What you say, eh boys? You think him or the dog's be smelling the most high?"

The other Frenchies in town was all on the dog's side; they admitted that he wasn't nearly so hogo as Albert Godspeed, so Albert and Couteau had to fight. That was part of the decorations too. The champions always fought at least once before they went off into the bush. It gave folks a chance to see who would be best to wager on.

They both fought with the natural weapon of that country. We called her the claw because she looked like nothing so much as a Shoshone paggamoggon with a great steel grizzly claw hooked on the end of her.

The claw was born in the mills, where we pulled slabs off the gangway with her, but she could no more stay in the mills

58

than gunpowder stayed in Chinese firecrackers. Men-folk first started using her as a weapon when the governor went and outlawed firearms, and just never gave her up once they found out how ugly they could be when they fought with her.

Albert had longer arms and he hooked out Reginald's left eye like you'd spear an onion out of the pickle jar. The eyeball and the muscles dangled down Reginald's cheek and Reginald pretended he was about fit to die. That fooled Albert and he let down his guard enough to get one of his own eyes hooked out for his foolishness. Then they fought real mad for about fifteen minutes, as desperate and turtle-brained as two bull moose with locked horns stomping one another as they starve to death. When we finally got them apart they was both blind in one eye and gouged over the rest of their bodies like a pair of fir logs bouncing out of a Fraser River canyon.

That first fight was in early June. By the end of July the hate was so thick you could taste it in your kalia. That's Finnish beer, and most of the time it tastes like ale, only a lot weaker; but then it was bitter and burnt, like someone had spitten tobacco into it. Them fights didn't usually get that bitter; sometimes they was even funny.

But the only funny thing that happened that summer was a Yankee hunter that came up with some men looking for grizzly, and even that wasn't too funny after a while. We had a lot of fun watching him trying to get Broken Bear's Indians to guide him to a grizzly. The Indians didn't really know where they come from or where they was going by then. They worshipped rifles as much as totems, and whisky more than either. But one thing they still figured was that some time in the past they had been related to the grizzlies, and they still called them "the bears that walk like men". The Yankee wasted a lot of rifles and a lot more whisky before he realized that none of those Indians was going to guide him to a grizzly.

He trapped a guide, though. He was a slick little claim-jumper. He spent two days drinking with Godspeed, then he went to talk to Reginald. He told Reginald that Albert claimed all Frenchies was too soft to help him locate his traps, and scared like little salmon of grizzlies anyhow. Reginald went off to guide him without even telling the foreman.

He come back after a couple of weeks, though. He come back swearing that the Yankee couldn't catch the buttons on his breeches. He thought the Yankee meant to shoot the bear like any normal hunter would, and the thought of trying to move a six-hundred-pound grizzly from a pit into a cage frightened him more than twenty Alberts. The Yankee never told anyone he meant to take the grizzly alive for a zoo.

The Yankee came back about the end of August and we had to give him the last laugh. He had three of them big bears locked up in cages and had only lost one of the men he had brought along with him. He told us he figured he'd stay around and take some of our money to carry off home with our bears.

On the twelfth of September, the night of the last quarter of the moon, we took Albert and Reginald up to the chance tree up by the Minassi's forks. That was another of the decorations. The champions had to toss axes at the chance tree to see who would get to head off first into the bush. We was wagering, but you could see a lot of men would rather be laying out fists than dollars. The hate was so strong I could see it hurling into the woods around us the way those mongrel curs in Double Mont will hurl themselves after a crippled dog, all teeth and no kindness.

The wagering didn't go too high on the axe-throwing. We was waiting for later. Reginald won and he picked Burnt Pine Valley for the fighting place. He also picked to be the first to head off. The foreman of last year's winning camp gave both Reginald and Albert a leather sack with eight gold guineas.

That was the main decoration. Each champion had to lay one of those guineas at the base of Burnt Pine every day without getting killed or maimed or caught. You could play it any way you wanted, from hide-an-seek, to duelling, to ambush and murdering. Once Reginald was gone, with his claw in one hand and his guineas in the other, we put a watch over Albert and settled down to the real wagering. The Yankee was taking almost any odds on Reginald, so we figured he either knew something or was turtle-brained from hunting those grizzlies. He let the odds go up to eight to one, then we knew he was turtle-brained, and even some of the folks from Reginald's camp began to bet against Reginald.

Reginald went walking through the wilderness as though he owned it. He walked all night and at dawn he scratched his first claw mark on the bark of the Burnt Pine. The tree was burnt on one side from lightning, but the other side was still surviving. Reginald laid the whole sack of guineas on one of the burnt limbs. Then he went back to one of the grizzly pits he had helped the Yankee build and got it ready for Albert Godspeed.

He let himself down with a rope he had carefully concealed around his belly and carefully hauled out all the cedar boughs placed there to break the bear's fall. Then he cut the supports so they would give way when a man stepped on them, and climbed out. He hid the boughs in the bush and patched the hole in the pit. He covered the hole with pine needles and spread more around the edges. By that time even he was having trouble finding where the pit ended and the trail began, for there were weeds growing in the soil the Yankee had spread over the pit and the whole area was covered with a layer of darkening fir needles and yellow leaves.

When he was sure Albert couldn't see the pit, he made himself a camp to the right of it. He built a blind, gathered a supply of blueberries, started a few fish lines, and set a gut-string rabbit trap. He didn't build a fire that night because he knew Albert would hang up on the rim of the valley until dawn made it safe for him to come down, and from up there even a child could spot a night fire. All night he huddled in the boughs from the bear pit and waited for the dawn.

Albert knew a lot about the bush for an Englishman. He walked down the trail with his head high, for he knew that a man rushing out of the bush would be an easy target for him as long as he kept his own feet planted on the ground. He knew the whiskey-jacks and chipmunks would warn him if Reginald came sneaking towards him through the bush. He knew which berries to eat and which to leave alone. Yet after a time his eye blinked at every small noise or sudden silence, and flickered at the trees around him as if he were looking for a place to scurry into. He knew that men had been known to take a chance on throwing away their claw if they figured they could end the battle with one blow that way. He began to shake beneath his shoulders, the early morning winds chilled him, and his hands were unfriendly as he rubbed them against his cheeks for warmth. He slouched, and soon he was hulking along the trail like a Cree on foot in a Blackfoot prairie; wondering if any of the knives that bit him would be sharpened with kindness and kill quickly; pretending there was no danger, pretending he would escape, but never preventing the fear from settling in him, never preventing it from turning his eye wary and cruel as any skunk bear's.

So he could make excuses for not seeing the pit, because no one had warned him about that, and he was imagining what his fear would drive him to do to the other eye of Reginald Couteau, and he was watching both sides of the trail as he had been told, and the pit was so covered with layers of living and dead plants that the Yankee himself might have fallen into it; but when he fell he broke his left leg on the hard, gravelly earth which lined the pit, and he could make no excuse for that.

Reginald came out from the blind and stared down into the pit. He stroked his moustaches like a duckhunter waiting for his dog to retrieve the game. He was frightened when he heard the moans but he relaxed when he had pushed away the broken supports and could see Albert's leg lying crooked away from him like slash beneath a toppled pine tree. He laughed and wondered if a man would die by nature in eight days with such a wound or if he would have to help the old woman along.

"Hey Anglais! You do pretty stupid damn thing, eh what?" he shouted, trying to imitate Albert's limey talking.

The moaning stopped and nothing else came along, so Reginald peered down to see if Albert was dead. He couldn't tell. He peered around the edge. He was a little itchy, but not about what he had done; he had obeyed all the rules, no one could blame him; but he wanted to make sure Albert was dead. He had once fooled Albert into letting his shield down, and he didn't want to fall for his own trick. He thought about lowering himself into the pit but thought against it. Even with a broken leg Albert would have one clear shot at him while he clambered down, and a thrown claw could be just as deadly as any other.

"Hey Anglais, you be dead down there?"

There was no reply, so he continued: "You too much of skunk bear to stand on the feet, eh! I fix you very good, eh?"

Albert did not stir, so Reginald shucked off his sack and sat down on the trail to eat. He talked loudly to himself.

"Me, truly I don't have much of the problem. I only wait until you be dead like the duck then I go home and say I have not been seeing you ever, when I wait by the trail all the eight days. Even the idiot ones cannot be knowing how I made the trap. I only follow them out and watch them find your poor body all torn by some crows. How you like that idea, Anglais!"

But there was no answer from Albert. Reginald made sure there were no supports extending into the pit and that Albert had no rope. Then he went to check his traps and lines and try to puzzle out a solution to his problems. He decided the best thing would be to get up early in the morning, while

Albert was asleep or dead, and drop one of the big fir supports on his head.

He collected two trout and a rabbit, set the lines again, baited them with some of the rabbit meat, and then collected blueberries until it was almost dark. He cached the rabbit and the blueberries with his watersack in a nearby tree, baked the trout and ate them with some of his hardtack. After he had collected a large pile of firwood he scraped the leaves and needles away from his dinner fire and built a larger, warmth fire to last him the night. He was near enough to hear Albert if he came to and tried to dig his way out. Except for that he had no worries.

For a time he woke every hour to feed the fire, but after that it seemed to burn without his aid. For the rest of the night he ignored it, he was too sleepy to figure out why it kept burning, and towards morning he tumbled into a second pit. The smouldering support which had given way under him sparked the cedar boughs into flame and he gave himself quite a burn trying to put them out.

When he had the fire all stomped into ashes he cursed his god, then himself, then the Yankee who had remarked foolishly one day to his helpers that the only way to capture an animal who avoids traps built on his trail is to build one just off it. Then he shut up so that Albert wouldn't realize he was caught in one of his own pits. The Englishman kind of had an ear for the sound of crashing supports, though, and having decided that Reginald was no longer in a position to be tricked, he laughed loudly despite the pain it caused him.

"I say there, Frenchie! You put your foot in your mouth and swallowed it, boot and all. Christ! I haven't laughed so hard since the time we put the moose in your cookshack."

Albert soon laughed his pride out. He knew he wouldn't last a week without help of some sort. His leg seemed to be running away inside and part of the time he wasn't sure if he was faking unconscious or if it was faking him. He knew Reginald could dig a path up the side of the pit in three or four days unless he was hurt.

It wasn't a very hard idea for Reginald to reach. There was a grizzly roaming that domain who had dug himself out of several of those traps. It only took him a day or two, but he had an eighteen-foot arm-spread to make things easier. After the first fright of being trapped had worn off he almost let the traps do his hunting for him. There was usually at least one full of a great thrashing bull moose. The bear was already nearly fat enough for his winter sleep. Reginald Couteau was at least as smart as that bear. He shouted out at Albert.

"Hey, you give me three, four day, *petit chien,* and I be dug out of here. Then you laugh through both sides of the mouth because I come split it from one ear to the other."

But misery is a sad partner, and by the end of the day they had ceased to hurl curses at each other. Albert could tell from the slow sounds of digging and the odd moan that Reginald was hurt. Reginald realized that with his rope and his food left above him and the burns on his hands and ankles blistering, he would not get out without help of some sort. In the morning, after they had both shivered fireless through the night, they began to talk.

"You know, Frenchie, this whole damn war is rather absurd. You ever hear who started it?"

"No, but I think it must have been a Frenchie," said Reginald Couteau as quietly as he could make himself.

"Not on your life. Must have been a bullheaded Englishman."

"You have the trouble for to get the patch for the eye, Albert?"

"No, I got the harness-maker to cut me out about six all at once. How about you?"

"*Oui,* I have the trouble. It must be that I should have been asking the harness-maker myself."

"Ought to have told me, Reg. I would have given you a few."

"Say, Albert, might it be that you give me some of the

hardtack? This digging make me very tired."

"Sorry, old boy, but I have just enough to last me until the men come and haul me out of here."

"You think maybe you be last so long?"

"Perhaps."

They left it at that for another day until both were becoming weak and feverish; then Reginald swallowed and asked:

"Eh Albert! Suppose if I promised not to make you wounded when I get out?"

"Suppose that you go plumb to the devil."

"Well, suppose then that I help you to get out or tell the men where they be finding you."

"I suppose that might be, that. You tell them where they'll find me, where they be *find*ing me."

"Good, then we have settled it. Only one piece of hardtack. And some sip of water."

"I don't carry water to where the streams are."

"Tabernac, I cannot eat the bread without some water."

"But I do have a small bottle of whisky."

"Can you throw it over here without you break the bottle?"

"That's not the question. Can you throw your claw over here without you break the me?"

"*Oui,* I can do that. You keep to talk and I wind it in my shirt and throw it over. Then you put the whisky in my shirt and throw it back."

They practised for a while with hunks of cedar, then made the exchange. After that they lay in their pits a shade more contented, one with both claws, the other with some whisky and some hardtack, and both with the warming prospect of getting home.

Reginald dug more easily now. He kept Albert awake during the night so that he could talk while he dug. He broke open the worst of the blisters and poured a little whisky on them. They told each other lies about the women they had known and the trees they had crowned until it was almost dawn. Then they made a pact to end the feud and get a legend started about themselves. Albert Godspeed and Reginald Couteau, they would be known far and wide as the two great peacemakers of the wilderness. They tossed the bottle back and forth to drink on it. What with the hope and the whisky and the new friendship they was both quite gay when they hear a figure crashing around near the trail. They both ran to the far sides of their pits but they couldn't see much except the morning mist which rose even to the tops of the brushy hills around Burnt Pine Valley.

"Hey, someone comes, eh, Frenchie?"

"*Oui, Anglais,* it is *grand Jean* from the camp of me. Only a man so big could make so big the noise."

"No, Frenchie, no such luck. It's one of Broken Bear's young braves. I told him to send someone after me if I didn't leave a mark on the edge of the feud area every day. He's still a mite upset about the condition you left his daughter in. I'm sure he will not mind leaving you here to rot."

"*Non, non, petit chien,* you hope for too much. Me, I would know the step of *grand Jean* anywhere. It is many times that I have gone through the woods with him. When I leave here with him we will drop one of those supports through the other eye of you. He will be glad to see you die. He will remember all the wars between your fathers and ours."

The grizzly had held off for two days because the smell of man was so strong. He had a flattened bullet nose in his haunch and a trap-mangled right paw to keep caution in him, but he was hungry now so he forgot them.

The traps had ruined him to a certain degree. Before, he would have fled from any odour of man but now he had learned to overcome it. Each of the stinking traps saved him the trouble of hunting. Once they had rid him of a hostile bear that wanted to take over his domain; often they held large bull moose, and now and then a buck deer.

The men in the pits started shouting as the noise drew nearer.

"Eh Jean! I have captured us a fine Englishman for to drop pine logs upon."

"Broken Bear! Broken Bear! A case of Hudson's Bay whisky if you forget that noise in the other pit."

"Eh Jean, pour nous nous divertons, nous lui écraserons avec les roches."

The bear stopped once at a large blueberry bush and once at a rotten log. He picked the bush clean, then overturned the log and laid his arm alongside it. When enough ants had scurried onto the arm he lifted it and licked them off the fur. He left the ants and ambled slowly towards the traps. There was a large stream full of silvery trout jumping in the misty waters but he ignored them. The grizzly went faster and stronger with each crashing, unmolested step he took.

That was how he told it, my grandfather, to me and Stephen and Shreve and Louis and Farley, seated with open eyes around his wrinkled old figure; watching him stir the embers up into a fire again, then, when he had it blazing, place his black bowler on his head and stare back at us.

"Some people," he said, "find out about this land as quick as a fresh-born bear cub finds his mama's teat. Some people take longer than a starving wolf running down a deer and die before they really find out. It's big and it'll take a lot of man's hogo'd ideas, a lot of sickness and laziness and war, but try and trot them in here by the freight-car load and it'll let them bloat their funny weak bodies until they can't fly and then lift an arm and crush them in their own blood-fat greed."

And we, too afraid to ask him questions, stared at the fire, or perhaps we had no need to ask him questions, perhaps we were part already of the mukluks and the bowler and the tales; perhaps part already even of the wrinkled face and shimmering eyes — so that secretly at night we had to stare at ourselves in mirrors to make sure that we were not getting smiling wrinkles under our eyes; not wearing our hats as though they were a present from a queen; not remembering the day we had finally captured Henri La Mort on the shores of Great Bear Lake after more than two years of trailing.

BUSHED
Earle Birney

He invented a rainbow but lightning struck it
shattered it into the lake-lap of a mountain
so big his mind slowed when he looked at it

Yet he built a shack on the shore
learned to roast porcupine belly and
wore the quills on his hatband

At first he was out with the dawn
whether it yellowed bright as wood-columbine
or was only a fuzzed moth in a flannel of storm
But he found the mountain was clearly alive
sent messages whizzing down every hot morning
boomed proclamations at noon and spread out
a white guard of goat
before falling asleep on its feet at sundown

When he tried his eyes on the lake   ospreys
would fall like valkyries
choosing the cut-throat
He took then to waiting
till the night smoke rose from the boil of the sunset

But the moon carved unknown totems
out of the lakeshore
owls in the beardusky woods derided him
moosehorned cedars circled his swamps and tossed
their antlers up to the stars
then he knew   though the mountain slept   the winds
were shaping its peak to an arrowhead
poised

And now he could only
bar himself in and wait
for the great flint to come singing into his heart

PROGRESSIVE INSANITIES OF A PIONEER
Margaret Atwood

I

He stood, a point
on a sheet of green paper
proclaiming himself the centre,

with no walls, no borders
anywhere; the sky no height
above him, totally un-
enclosed
and shouted:

Let me out!

II

He dug the soil in rows,
imposed himself with shovels.

He asserted
into the furrows, I
am not random.

The ground
replied with aphorisms:

a tree-sprout, a nameless
weed, words
he couldn't understand.

III

The house pitched
the plot staked
in the middle of nowhere.

At night the mind
inside, in the middle
of nowhere.

The idea of an animal
patters across the roof.

In the darkness the fields
defend themselves with fences
in vain:
  everything
  is getting in.

IV

By daylight he resisted.
He said, disgusted
with the swamp's clamourings and the outbursts
of rocks,
  This is not order
  but the absence
  of order.

He was wrong, the unanswering
forest implied:

  It was
  an ordered absence

V

For many years
he fished for a great vision,
dangling the hooks of sown
roots under the surface
of the shallow earth.

It was like
enticing whales with a bent
pin. Besides he thought

in that country
only the worms were biting.

VI

If he had known unstructured

space is a deluge
and stocked his log house-
boat with all the animals

even the wolves,

he might have floated.

But obstinate he
stated, The land is solid
and stamped,

watching his foot sink
down through stone
up to the knee.

VII

Things
refused to name themselves; refused
to let him name them.

The wolves hunted
outside.

On his beaches, his clearings,
by the surf of under-
growth breaking
at his feet, he foresaw
disintegration
                    and in the end
through eyes
made ragged by his
effort, the tension
between subject and object,

the green
vision, the unnamed
whale invaded.

AN ARTIST'S TABERNACLE

Emily Carr

September, 1935

Blessed camp life again! Sunshine pouring joyously through
the fringe of trees between the van and the sea. I got up very
early today. The earth dripped with dew. These September
days are fiercely hot in their middles and moistly cold at the
beginning and end. In spite of its fierce heat the sun could not
disperse the fog across the water all day yesterday. It hid the
mountains. All night and most of the day the fog-horn blared
dismally, each toot ending in a despairing groan.

There is a young moon early on in the evening, but she
goes off to wherever she does go and leaves the rest of the
night in thick velvety blackness, shades darker than closed
eyes and so thick you can take it in your hands and your teeth
can bite into it. When that is down upon the land one thinks
a lot about Italy and Ethiopia and wonders how things will
settle. One hangs on for dear life to the thought there is only
one God and He fills the universe, "comprehends all
substance, fills all space" and is "pure being by whom all
things be."

Life looks completely different after a good night's sleep. The
hips on the rose bushes never looked so brilliant nor the light
through the trees so sparkly. Breakfast cooked on the oil stove
in the van and eaten tucked up in my bed with the window
and the world on my right and the row of dogs in their boxes,
still sleeping, on the left. Sheep and roosters crying, "Good
morning, God, and thank you," and the fog-horn booing the
fog out of existence, making it sneak off in thin, shamefaced
white streaks.

There will be sunshine in the woods today, and mosquitoes
and those sneaky "no-see-ums", that have not the honest buzz
of the mosquito that invites you to kill him. You neither see
nor hear nor feel "no-see-ums" till you go to bed that night,
then all the venom the beast has pricked into your flesh starts
burning and itching and nearly drives you mad.

Sketching in the big woods is wonderful. You go, find a space wide enough to sit in and clear enough so that the undergrowth is not drowning you. Then, being elderly, you spread your camp stool and sit and look round. "Don't see much here." "Wait." Out comes a cigarette. The mosquitoes back away from the smoke. Everything is green. Everything is waiting and still. Slowly things begin to move, to slip into their places. Groups and masses and lines tie themselves together. Colours you had not noticed come out, timidly or boldly. In and out, in and out your eye passes. Nothing is crowded; there is living space for all. Air moves between each leaf. Sunlight plays and dances. Nothing is still now. Life is sweeping through the spaces. Everything is alive. The air is alive. The silence is full of sound. The green is full of colour. Light and dark chase each other. Here is a picture, a complete thought, and there another and there . . .

There are themes everywhere, something sublime, something ridiculous, or joyous, or calm, or mysterious. Tender youthfulness laughing at gnarled oldness. Moss and ferns, and leaves and twigs, light and air, depth and colour chattering, dancing a mad joy-dance, but only apparently tied up in stillness and silence. You must be still in order to hear and see.

September 13th
How it has rained! With the canvas top of the van so close to my crown I have full opportunity to note all the different sounds: the big, bulgy drops that splash as they strike, the little pattery ones, the determined battalions of hurried ones coming with a rattling pelt, the soft gentle ones blessing everything, the cleansing and the slopping and the irritated fussy ones. It is amazing that no two of them sound alike when you listen. The moss and grass and earth are gulping it in. Every pot and pail in camp is overflowing. After the water shortage it seems so reckless to throw any away. Mists rush up

from the earth to meet the rain coming down so that between them both, the fog-horn is in a constant blither.

All the busy bustle has gone out of the wasps' wings. They drift in drearily seeking a warm corner to give up in. It is the third day of rain; everything is soggy and heavy now. Patches of bright green show in the faded, drab fields, and patches of pale gold are in the green of the maples. Colours are changing their places as in Musical Chairs to the tune of the rain. The fog-horn has a fat sound in the heavy air.

A dreary procession of turkeys is mincing down the road. The rain drips one end from their drooping tails and the other from their meek heads. There is no gobble left in the cock and even the pathetic peep of the hens is mute. If ever any beast had the right to be depressed it is the turkey, born for us to make merry over his carcass. The peep of the chicks and the hens is downcast, their walk funereal, their heavy flight bewildered. The cock tries to put a good face on it occasionally and denounces his fate with purple indignation, but you have only to "shoo!" and he collapses.

September 15th

From the window of the van, tucked up cosily with a hot bottle across my feet, I can sit and watch the angry elements. It has poured for five days, wholehearted, teeming rain. Today loud, boisterous wind is added. The sea is boiling over the black rocks; branches of foaming white smother them. Where there are no rocks to punish, it boils in wicked waves, row upon row that never catch up. The sheep and turkeys across the fields crop restlessly. They scatter and do not lie down. The waves and trees shout back at each other, a continuous roar and hubbub. Only in the van is there a spot of quiet. The dogs, monkey, and I are all in our beds in a row like links in a chain of peace. We are cuddled down listening with just a shell of canvas shutting out the turmoil.

It is very wonderful dumped here in its middle and yet not of it. Time was when I would have wanted to go out and be

buffeted, join in, hit back. Years change that wish —
rheumatics, sore joints, fat here and there, old-age fears and
distrust of one's capabilities. I am sorry about the work but I
haven't one doubt that it's all a part of the discipline and
training.

September 19th
The early morns are nippy, dewy, penetrating cold that won't
be denied admittance either to the van or to your person. It
ignores canvas and flesh and blood. It is after rheumatic joints
and dull livers. Last night I wasn't much removed from a
mollusc because I'd been behind myself pushing all day — real
liverish. It was not till 4 p.m. I got up steam and a real
enthusiasm over a bit of near woods. It seems an impossibility
to squeeze energy to walk the big wood distance. A
domineering liver is a fearsome thing.

When the horn, normal at first and developing into a
despairing grunt, informs the early world that fog is on land
and sea, van cosiness reaches its high-water mark. One effort
and you have clambered out of bunk. A match across the shelf
checks the horn back. Soon the sweet kettle song rises.
Toast-and-teaish odours skedaddle the fog. And there you are,
washed, ready, pillowed, hot-bottled, breakfasted, and full of
content.

I rose early and made tea and spent a delicious hour in bed,
luxuriating. The sun is penetrating through the woods now.
The green grey is coldly lit with a cool sparkle. How solemn
the pines look, more grey than green, a quiet spiritual grey,
blatant gaudiness of colours swallowed, only the beautiful
carrying power of grey, lifting into mystery. Colour holds,
binds, "enearths" you. When light shimmers on colours, folds
them round and round, colour is swallowed by glory and
becomes unspeakable. Paint cannot touch it, but until we have
absorbed and understood and become related to the glory
about us how can we be prepared for higher? If we did not
have longings there would be nothing to satisfy.

Yesterday I went into a great forest, I mean a portion of growth undisturbed for years and years. Way back, some great, grand trees had been felled, leaving their stumps with the ragged row of "screamers" in the centre, the last chords to break, chords in the tree's very heart. Growth had repaired all the damage and hidden the scars. There were second-growth trees, lusty and fine, tall-standing bracken and sword ferns, salal, rose and blackberry vines, useless trees that nobody cuts, trees ill-shaped and twisty that stood at the foot of those mighty arrow-straight monarchs long since chewed by steel teeth in the mighty mills, chewed into utility, nailed into houses, churches, telephone poles, all the "woodsyness" extracted, nothing remaining but wood.

And so it must be. Everything has to teach something else growth and development. Even the hideous wars are part of the growth and development. Who knows? It may be that the great and strong are killed to give the shrivelled weaklings their chance. We just don't know anything. We can only trust and grow as straight as we can like the trees.

The world would laugh at these "pencil thinkings", but they help one to think, reach conclusions. Our minds are a mess of "begun" thoughts, little abortive starts. Another twitch and we are off on another thought leaving them all high and dry along the beaches because the waves of our thougts have not swept high enough to pick them up again. Perhaps a full tide with big waves will come later and refloat them and carry them to another beach and on and on till they stick somewhere and their elements turn into something else. Nothing ever, ever stands still and we never, never catch up. One daren't think about it too much for it makes one giddy.

When the early morning nip is blueing your nose, and "Little Smelly" is tuning up the tea kettle, and the van windows have modesty blinds of steam, and the air is too full of vapour for the wasp wings to have any buzz and you hope their stings also are waterlogged, then it is good to pin a yesterday's sketch up and look it squarely in the face. Um! It did not look so bad in last night's light. It is done in swirly rings. Why? Not for affectation any more than the cubists squared for affectation. Like them I was trying to get planes but used disks instead of cubes. It gives a swirling, lively movement, but until mitigated is too blatant. Things are swirling by themselves. The thing to do now is to swirl them together into one great movement. That is going to be a thrilling canvas to work out in the studio later, refining, co-ordinating, if there is money enough to buy paints. Why worry? Here the job is to absorb. What, eat the woods? Yes, as one eats the sacrament. Munching of the bread is not eating the sacrament; it is feeding on it in our hearts by faith with thanksgiving. It is good for remembrance.

Bads and goods have hurled themselves with velocity through this day. The lamp went on the blink. The kettle broke. Woo got the salt bottle when I was out, threw the top down the bank, and filled the bottle with bugs. In a moment of emphasis I waved the iodine bottle to bring home a point and deluged Mrs. McMuir, arms, dress, floor, and it won't wash off. Then I clambered up a ladder to paint the lid of the old lady and waterproof her for winter; the little devils of dogs, seeing me well set, took the lid off the meat pot and devoured today's and tomorrow's dinner. And I got a cheque for $15 for a sketch I never expected to materialize. Burned my melba in the McMuirs' oven. Came home and found the Yates girls had left a lamp wick and some good prune plums on the van step. All in one day. Such is life.

Splendid days, cold and hot; gold, grey; soft, crisp. Any hour any condition may prevail. The woods are tender one minute and austere the next, sometimes riotously rich, coldly pale in colour. I did two studies yesterday in thick, wild undergrowth. At the beginning of each I dropped into a merry swing-off and ended in a messy conglomeration, but there are thoughts in them to follow up. They swing a little but not in

one sublime swinging "go". Something keeps peeping out;
look at it and it's gone.

Most men are very stupid. You ask a perfectly clear, straight
question, "Can I go through your gate up into the woods to
sketch?" He looks at you, closes the gate, looks over the top,
grins foolishly, weighs himself first on one foot and then on
the other, and says, "I don't know. It would not be any good
to you."

"Why?"

"Well, you see . . . What do you want?"

"To pass through the gate and get up the bank on to those
rocks."

Again he went through all his silly manoeuvres. "It
wouldn't be any good," he said again. "There's a high barbed
fence. You could not get through."

Stupid ass, why didn't he say so right off!

The schoolhouse is at the top of the hill. A rough
playground is scooped out of the trees and brush. It looks
dull. Not a sound comes out of the open windows. The door
is fast shut, and there are jam bottles holding a few scrubby
flowers on the high window-ledges. There are two swings, two
rings, and two privies. I'd hate to be educated there. At the
corner, the hill takes a nasty curve. The gravel is rough and
twists ankles. The man's barbed wire fence has turned and
runs up through the jungle. Now one can turn in among the
salal bushes. The sheep have made walks there. Their hooves
have cut the rotten fallen logs where they cross. The earth is
damp and reddish brown. Mostly it is thickly spread with
coarse herbage and fallen trees rich with moss, tough salal
with fat black berries walking single file up their stalks like
Chinamen, strong naked roots veining the red earth like old
knotted hands. There are a few birds but all the woods are
mostly hushed and mysterious. When a squirrel coughs and
when wrens hop among the twigs, it makes one jump. The

big sword ferns point up in imitation of the high-pointed pines.

A hundred yards farther on the road is lost. The forest has closed about you. You will see neither beast nor man unless you keep to the little sheep trail. It is all above your head, the tangle, and there is no place for your feet for the rotted tree boles that lie waist high, hidden in scrub so that you cannot perceive them. There is the next generation of pines, cedars, hemlocks; uprooted tree-roots as high as a house, the earth clinging to them still, young trees and bushes growing among them and the hole the tree left filled now with vigorous green. You need not penetrate far into this massed tangle. Here is a little stream's dried-up bed. Across it the tangle rises, the sheep path goes up. You can sit on the path and look down on the snarl of green. It is lovely. Suddenly, its life envelops you, living, moving, surging with being, palpitating with overpowering, terrific life, life, life.

November 28th
Working on jungle. How I want to get that thing! Have not succeeded so far but it fascinates. What most attracts me in those wild, lawless, deep, solitary places? First, nobody goes there. Why? Few have anything to go *for*. The loneliness repels them, the density, the unsafe hidden footing, the dank smells, the great quiet, the mystery, the general mix-up (tangle, growth, what may be hidden there), the insect life. They are repelled by the awful solemnity of the age-old trees, with the wisdom of all their years of growth looking down upon you, making you feel perfectly infinitesimal — their overpowering weight, their groanings and creakings, mutterings and sighings — the rot and decay of the old ones — the toadstools and slugs among the upturned, rotting roots of those that have fallen, reminding one of the perishableness of even those slow-maturing, much-enduring growths. No, to the average woman and to the average man (unless he goes

there to kill, to hunt, or to destroy the forest for utility), the forest jungle is a closed book. In the abstract people may say they love it but they do not prove it by entering it and breathing its life. They stay outside and talk about its beauty. This is bad for them but it is good for the few who do enter because the holiness and quiet is unbroken.

Sheep and other creatures have made a few trails. It will be best to stick to these. The salal is tough and stubborn, rose and blackberry thorny. There are the fallen logs and mossy stumps, the thousand varieties of growth and shapes and obstacles, the dips and hollows, hillocks and mounds, riverbeds, forests of young pines and spruce piercing up through the tangle to get to the quiet light diluted through the overhanging branches of great overtopping trees. Should you sit down, the great, dry, green sea would sweep over and engulf you. If you called out, a thousand echoes would mock back. If you wrestle with the growth it will strike back. If you listen it will talk, if you jabber it will shut up tight, stay inside itself. If you *let* yourself get "creepy", creepy you can be. If you face it calmly, claiming relationship, standing honestly before the trees, recognizing one Creator of you and them, one life pulsing through all, one mystery engulfing all, then you can say with the Psalmist who looked for a place to build a tabernacle to the Lord, I "found it in the hills and in the fields of the wood."

TUNDRA
Farley Mowat

Sprawled across the upper mainland of Canada lies a tremendous tract of treeless tundra plains that, for centuries, has been known to people of European stock as the Barren Grounds, the Barren Lands, or simply the Barrens. In recent times North Americans have tended to ignore this almost limitless expanse of sea and land, except to think of it as a frozen treasure-house of natural resources.

It has not always been so. Until fifty or sixty years ago the Arctic was a living reality to North Americans of every walk of life. It had become real, and it stayed real for them, because men of their own kind were daring its remote fastnesses in search of pure adventure, unprotected by the elaborate mechanical shields that we now demand whenever we step out of our heated sanctuaries. Press and magazines followed the fortunes of these men with a good deal more honest enthusiasm than that with which they now follow the exploits of space travelers. Personal accounts of Arctic voyages and journeys lined the shelves of bookshops. Those who stayed at home identified themselves with Arctic travelers, as they can no longer truly identify themselves with the mechanical heroes of modern times.

The mainland tundra of Canada embraces almost 500,000 *square miles* of naked, rolling, lake-dotted plains, broken here and there by ranges of worn-down hills and vast regions of frost-shattered grey rock and gravels. To an observer in a small aircraft droning over it for endless hours, the tundra seems to be almost as much a world of water as of land. Its lakes, ponds, and rivers are beyond counting. Seen from the air, the land between appears to be dun-colored, monochromatic, apparently featureless, reaching to the horizon on all sides with an illusion of terrible monotony.

This is strictly an illusion. Look closer and the void of land and water becomes an intricate and living mosaic, varied and colourful. The multitudes of tundra ponds are shallow and reflect the pale northern skies in every shade of blue and violet or, discolored by the organic stains of muskeg water, they become sepia, burnished copper, burning red, or shimmering green. The numberless rivers run no straight courses but twist tortuously through chocolate-brown muskegs or between silver-grey ridges of stone and gravel (moraines of vanished glaciers), or compete in patternmaking with the meandering embankments of sandy eskers (casts of dead rivers that once flowed under the melting ice sheet). Some eskers roam for hundreds of miles and bear a disconcerting resemblance to the constructions of a long-forgotten race of manic giants.

Viewed by a summer traveler on the ground, the tundra gives the feeling of limitless space, intensified until one wonders if there can be any end to this terrestrial ocean whose waves are the rolling ridges. Perhaps nowhere else in the world, except far out at sea, does a man feel so exposed. On this northern prairie it is as if the ceiling of the world no longer exists and no walls remain to close one in.

In winter this sea simile gains even greater weight, for then both land and water vanish, blending into one impassive sweep of frozen undulations that seems to have no shore.

Why these mighty plains should have been called "barren" is hard to understand. Even if the word is only intended to mean treeless, it is not entirely valid. Along the entire southern fringe, known as the taiga, there are trees — small and stunted, it is true, but trees. And scattered over the southern half of the northern prairies are islands of timber. One of these, on the Thelon River and almost dead centre in the plains, forms a timbered oasis 40 or 50 miles in length, with some single trees growing 30 feet in height. If "barren" is meant to mean barren of life, it is a gross misnomer. True, in winter there is not much life to be seen, but in summer the tundra is vividly alive.

For the most part the land is covered with a rich carpet of mosses, lichens, grasses, sedges, and dwarf shrubbery. The flowers are small, many of them minute, but they grow in fantastic abundance. Even on the naked ridges and on the frost-riven graveyards of broken stone that lie between some of the muskeg valleys, there is brilliant life; the rocks glow with the splashed kaleidoscope of lichens in 100 shades.

Animate life is just as abundant. The ponds, muskegs, and lakes are the breeding grounds for ducks, geese, and wading birds. The dry tundra and the rock tundra are the habitat of the northern grouse called ptarmigan, and of innumerable other birds. Snowy owls nest on the grassy flats and rough-legged hawks and falcons share the pale sky with the uncompromising raven which, almost alone among Arctic animals, refuses to change his color when winter whiteness obliterates the world. The waters of the larger lakes (those that do not freeze to the bottom in winter) and, in summer, the rivers too are full of whitefish, lake trout (40-pounders are not uncommon), suckers, and a flamboyant and peculiar fish — a distant relative of the trout — called grayling.

It is the mammals that dominate the land. During the peak periods of their cycles, short-tailed, mouselike lemmings are so abundant that one can hardly walk across the sedge and moss without sending them scuttling clumsily from underfoot. They provide the chief food of the white fox, whose cycle of abundance is keyed to theirs. Lemmings know nothing about birth control. They breed so prolifically that every four or five years they literally eat and crowd themselves out of house and home and then must either die or migrate elsewhere — and such migrations are fatal for most of them.

Even squirrels live on the tundra — gaudy, orange-colored ground squirrels that den in the sandy eskers or on dry gravel ridges, where the perpetual frost does not deny them entry to the ground.

The great white wolves, once abundant but now reduced to rare and scattered families, display an amiable curiosity, visiting human campsites to sit with cocked ears as they watch the inscrutable activities of men.

One of the most impressive of all the tundra beasts is the great brown bear called the Barren Land grizzly. Only a few decades ago this shambling giant roamed over most of the mainland tundra west of Hudson Bay, but now, like so many other species that have roused our murderous appetites, he has become so rare as almost to be just a memory.

Equally strange is the musk-ox — a black, stolid beast that looks like a cross between a bull and a huge shaggy goat (actually it is related, distantly, to both). Slow and placid but armed with sweeping horns, the musk-oxen have evolved the tactic of forming a hollow square when threatened. Because of their fine, underlying wool, the wildest winter weather cannot affect them. They have no real enemies save man, and in other times they called almost the entire tundra, both on the mainland and on the islands, home. But by the mid-twenties they had been exterminated from most of their range.

By far the most impressive of all the tundra beasts is the caribou. Caribou have literally provided the lifeblood of the human residents of the northern plains and of the taiga since time immemorial. These cousins of the reindeer formerly existed in such huge herds that they approached in numbers the buffalo of the southern prairies and probably outnumbered any of the great herd beasts of Africa. When Europeans first arrived on the edge of the northern prairie there may have been as many as five million caribou. Caribou and their predators, chiefly wolves and the native peoples, had lived together in balance for uncounted ages. We changed all that. In 1949 after Ottawa had finally taken notice of the terrible destruction of these northern deer, an aerial survey showed that only about 650,000 remained alive. By 1955 there were estimated to be about 280,000. By 1960 there were estimated to be fewer than 250,000, most of them west of Hudson Bay.

Men came early to the tundra plains. Along the ancient gravel beaches that now cling crazily to hillsides 300 feet above the shrunken levels of existing lakes, quartz flakes lie in profusion, and the broken points made by clumsy or unlucky workmen keep them company. They are as fresh-appearing now as when men gave them their present form, for no leaves have fallen to bury them in detritus; and the long winters have covered them with nothing more permanent than snow.

Little is known about these firstcomers except that they were plains dwellers; probably reindeer hunters out of the Asian north who may have entered the American continent along the narrow defile of tundra lying between the Brooks Range in Alaska and the polar sea.

Over the centuries new waves of nomads entered these Arctic prairies until, by about 1700, the tundra seems to have been mainly held by Eskimos of an ancient inland culture, while to the south of them, in the thin border forest of the taiga, people of Athapascan race (notably the Chipewyan, Copper, and Dog-Rib Indians) lived apart.

Early in the 18th century all this began to change. White traders had appeared on the southern prairies, bringing guns which they traded to the southern plains Indians. These people, mostly of Cree stock, began to wage modern war with their new weapons and they brought great pressure to bear on the taiga people, who were then armed only with bows, spears, and slings. Within a very few years this pressure drove the Athapascan Indians right out onto the open tundra and into bitter conflict with the inland Eskimos. Then the Chipewyans, in their turn, made contact with the white men and got guns, and soon they drove the tundra Eskimos into the most northerly reaches of the land.

This was how things stood when Europeans first approached the borders of the Barren Grounds. The tundra was not empty then, for it knew the comings and goings of many men — of men who were able to live there, and who did live there, because the land was bountiful.

It was a manifold bounty, including the fishes in the innumerable lakes, the tremendous flocks of ducks and geese, the hare, ptarmigan, musk-ox, Barren Land grizzly and, what was all important, the seemingly limitless herds of caribou.

But it was a bounty that was not destined to survive the rapacity of European man. In a world where all creatures — both beasts and men — had been in balance, the arrival of the intruders from across the eastern ocean brought chaos and destruction.

When I first visited the edge of the Barrens in 1935, it still retained at least the illusion of being a living land. I visited it again in 1947, 1948, and 1953, and during those years I saw life failing fast. Then in 1966 I flew across the entire breadth and depth of the tundra plains. The aircraft flew low over the open face of the country, and little was hidden from our eyes. Where, *during my own lifetime,* there had been as many as a million caribou, there were now only pathetic and scattered remnants. Where, *during my own lifetime,* scores of places had harbored many hundreds of human beings, now there were only crumbling cabins and abandoned camps. The circles of stones that marked the vanished tents of Indians and Eskimos stared eyeless and void beside the mute symbolic piles of stones raised by a vanished people who called them *inukok* — semblance of a man.

Westward to Great Slave Lake 500 miles from the coast of Hudson Bay, southward from the Arctic coast 600 miles across the plains into the thin forests almost to Reindeer Lake, *there were no human beings living in the land.* Nearly 300,000 square miles lay drained of human life and, to a great extent, of caribou, wolves, and other beasts who, like the people of the Arctic plains, had been dependent on the caribou for their survival. Truly this seemed to be the Barren Grounds.

As we flew over that endless desolation, I wondered if the great plains were doomed to remain no more than a monument to the terrible destructiveness of modern man. I wondered if we had turned our backs forever upon the *terre sterile* we had created.

In 1967 Canada entered her second century. Her first was 100 years of despoilment of natural life in a new and virgin world, and nowhere is this more bleakly demonstrated than in the North. The entire Arctic, once pregnant with life, has now become a hungry desert where not even the surviving

Eskimos can take sustenance solely from the land and from the sea. Having destroyed the natural-life environment of this gigantic region, men can now survive there only as aliens, dependent for food and clothing, fuel and shelter, on what is brought in from the world outside.

In Canada's second century we have the chance to undo some of the brutal, tragic errors of the past. If we turn northward again in imagination and in reality we can bring a dead world back to life, and we can share that life and be the richer for it.

All across the sweep of Asiatic tundra such a restoration has already been undertaken. Aboriginal Arctic peoples "farm" the Soviet tundra, where the first cousins of the caribou, the reindeer, now graze the Arctic prairies and provide protein-hungry peoples with millions of pounds of good meat every year. The Asian tundra, once as despoiled as ours and very nearly as moribund, is again a place of life for men and beasts. It can be done. In Canada's North, the remnant populations of Indians and Eskimos are almost without exception dependent for survival on relief and welfare as a result of the destruction of their old world. They could reoccupy that world; could find new, vigorous lives for themselves; could recolonize what is now one of the largest deserted regions on the planet. Musk-ox, caribou perhaps, but reindeer certainly, could bring life out of death; and the Arctic

seas could, with care and under the hands of reason, also regain their vitality, to provide a useful and modern way of life for the seal and walrus hunters now clustered in abject poverty in the handful of remaining settlements along our Arctic coasts.

In Canada's second century we could restore to life a portion of our country amounting to nearly a quarter of its total area, if we so willed. With ordinary human courage, endurance, and hardihood, tempered by compassion for and understanding of the natural world of the North, we may still reclaim the wasteland we have created in the Arctic.

The vital word is *reclaim:* to restore a ravaged land which is of such fragility that even the most minor blunders we have perpetrated on it in the past brought great disasters. However — and mark this well — *we will not reclaim the Arctic by waging a new war of greedy exploitation against it!* We will not restore it to life by turning from the rape of its living elements to the rape of its essential guts. If there is one immutable fact about the Arctic's future it is that our present view of that vast land as little more than a grab bag of oil, minerals, chemicals, and hydroelectric power will be absolutely fatal to it. If it is to become nothing more than one further sacrifice to the bitch goddess of technical progress, then it is irrevocably doomed.

I have my own vision of the high North. I envision it being transformed — restored — into a symbol of sanity in a world where madness is becoming the accepted mode of action. I see it being rigidly protected as one vast sanctuary — a world inviolate — where men will walk softly and wield no big technological bludgeons. I see it as one of the few remaining regions where life, both human and nonhuman, can still be lived within the framework of the timeless harmonies that have existed since life began.

I have heard an oracle: if we who have brought such massive discord and such wasting sickness to this planet cannot bring an end to our blind orgy of destruction, then, most surely, shall we perish from the earth.

ESKIMO HUNTER (NEW STYLE)
Al Purdy

In terylene shirt and suspenders
sun glasses and binoculars
Peterborough boat and Evinrude motor
Remington rifle with telescope sight
making hot tea on a Coleman stove
scanning the sea and shore for anything
that moves and lives and breathes
and so betrays itself
one way or another
All we need in the line of further equipment
is a sexy blonde in a bikini
trailing her hand thru the sunlit water
maybe a gaggle of Hollywood photographers
snapping pictures and smoking
nationally advertised brands
Like bwana in Africa
pukka sahib in Bengal
staked out on a tree platform
a tethered goat underneath wailing
Papa Hemingway's bearded ghost on safari
or fishing for giant turtles in Pango Pango
                Maybe it is phony
(and all we're after is seal)
but over the skyline
where the bergs heave and glimmer
under the glacier's foot
or down the fiord's blue water
                even under the boat itself
anywhere the unhappened instant is
real blood
                death for someone or something
                and it's reassuringly old fashioned

QUIXOTE IN THE SNOW
Charles Lillard

A north wind, always that traveling
Wind, drums the door.
The reader is listening.
A wolf pauses at the meadow's edge
And quickly enters your heart.

Eastward, a bitch with heavy dugs rises.
Near the river, a bell tolls the hour:
A reminder of our lost wilderness,
Shouldering itself into the old warmth of this room.

DARK PINES UNDER WATER
Gwendolyn MacEwen

This land like a mirror turns you inward
And you become a forest in a furtive lake;
The dark pines of your mind reach downward,
You dream in the green of your time,
Your memory is a row of sinking pines.

Explorer, you tell yourself this is not what you came for
Although it is good here, and green;
You had meant to move with a kind of largeness,
You had planned a heavy grace, an anguished dream.

But the dark pines of your mind dip deeper
And you are sinking, sinking, sleeper
In an elementary world;
There is something down there and you want it told.

AFTER THE SIRENS
Hugh Hood

They heard the sirens first about four forty-five in the morning. It was still dark and cold outside and they were sound asleep. They heard the noise first in their dreams and, waking, understood it to be real.

"What is it?" she asked him sleepily, rolling over in their warm bed. "Is there a fire?"

"I don't know," he said. The sirens were very loud. "I've never heard anything like that before."

"It's some kind of siren," she said, "downtown. It woke me up."

"Go back to sleep!" he said. "It can't be anything."

"No," she said. "I'm frightened. I wonder what it is. I wonder if the baby has enough covers." The wailing was still going on. "It couldn't be an air-raid warning, could it?"

"Of course not," he said reassuringly, but she could hear the indecision in his voice.

"Why don't you turn on the radio," she said, "just to see? Just to make sure. I'll go and see if the baby's covered up." They walked down the hall in their pajamas. He went into the kitchen, turned on the radio, and waited for it to warm up. There was nothing but static and hum.

"What's that station?" he called to her. "Conrad, or something like that."

"That's 640 on the dial," she said, from the baby's room. He twisted the dial and suddenly the radio screamed at him, frightening him badly.

"This is not an exercise. This is not an exercise. This is not an exercise," the radio blared. *"This is an air-raid warning. This is an air-raid warning. We will be attacked in fifteen minutes. We will be attacked in fifteen minutes. This is not an exercise."* He recognized the voice of a local announcer who did an hour of breakfast music daily. He had never heard the man talk like that before. He ran into the baby's room while the radio shrieked behind him: *"We will be attacked in fifteen minutes. Correction. Correction. In fourteen minutes. In fourteen minutes. We will be attacked in fourteen minutes. This is not an exercise."*

"Look," he said, "don't ask me any questions, please, just do exactly what I tell you and don't waste any time." She stared at him with her mouth open. "Listen," he said, "and do exactly as I say. They say this is an air-raid and we'd better believe them." She looked frightened nearly out of her wits. "I'll look after you," he said; "just get dressed as fast as you can. Put on as many layers of wool as you can. Got that?"

She nodded speechlessly.

"Put on your woollen topcoat and your fur coat over that. Get as many scarves as you can find. We'll wrap our faces and hands. When you're dressed, dress the baby the same way. We have a chance, if you do as I say without wasting time." She ran off up the hall to the coat closet and he could hear her pulling things about.

"This will be an attack with nuclear weapons. You have thirteen minutes to take cover," screamed the radio. He looked at his watch and hurried to the kitchen and pulled a cardboard carton from under the sink. He threw two can openers into it and all the canned goods he could see. There were three loaves of bread in the breadbox and he crammed them into the carton. He took everything that was wrapped and solid in the refrigerator and crushed it in. When the carton was full he took a bucket which usually held a garbage bag, rinsed it hastily, and filled it with water. There was a plastic bottle in the refrigerator. He poured the tomato juice out of it and rinsed it and filled it with water.

"This will be a nuclear attack." The disc jockey's voice was cracking with hysteria. *"You have nine minutes, nine minutes to take cover. Nine minutes."* He ran into the dark hall and bumped into his wife who was swaddled like a bear.

"Go and dress the baby," he said. "We're going to make it, we've just got time. I'll go and get dressed." She was crying, but there was no time for comfort. In the bedroom he forced himself into his trousers, a second pair of trousers, two shirts, and two sweaters. He put on the heaviest, loosest jacket he owned, a topcoat, and finally his overcoat. This took him just under five minutes. When he rejoined his wife in the living room, she had the baby swaddled in her arms, still asleep.

"Go to the back room in the cellar, where your steamer trunk is," he said, "and take this." He gave her a flashlight which they kept in their bedroom. When she hesitated he said roughly, "Go on, get going."

"Aren't you coming?"

"Of course I'm coming," he said. He turned the radio up as far as it would go and noted carefully what the man said. *"This will be a nuclear attack. The target will probably be the aircraft company. You have three minutes to take cover."* He picked up the carton and balanced the bottle of water on it. With the other hand he carried the bucket. Leaving the kitchen door wide open, he went to the cellar, passed through the dark furnace room, and joined his wife.

"Put out the flashlight," he said, "We'll have to save it. We have a minute or two, so listen to me." They could hear the radio upstairs. *"Two minutes,"* it screamed.

"Lie down in the corner of the west and north walls," he said quickly. "The blast should come from the north if they hit the target, and the house will blow down and fall to the south. Lie on top of the baby and I'll lie on top of you!"

She cuddled the sleeping infant in her arms. "We're going to die right now," she said, as she held the baby closer to her.

"No, we aren't," he said, "we have a chance. Wrap the scarves around your face and the baby's, and lie down." She handed him a plaid woollen scarf and he tied it around his face so that only his eyes showed. He placed the water and food in a corner and then lay down on top of his wife, spreading his arms and legs as much as possible, to cover and protect her.

"Twenty seconds," shrieked the radio. *"Eighteen seconds. Fifteen."*

He looked at his watch as he fell. "Ten seconds," he said aloud. "It's five o'clock. They won't waste a megaton bomb on us. They'll save it for New York." They heard the radio crackle into silence and they hung onto each other, keeping their eyes closed tightly.

Instantaneously the cellar room lit up with a kind of glow they had never seen before, the earthen floor began to rock and heave, and the absolutely unearthly sound began. There was no way of telling how far off it was, the explosion. The sound seemed to be inside them, in their bowels; the very air itself was shattered and blown away in the dreadful sound that went on and on and on.

They held their heads down, hers pushed into the dirt, shielding the baby's scalp, his face crushed into her hair, nothing of their skin exposed to the glow, and the sound went on and on, pulsing curiously, louder than anything they had ever imagined, louder than deafening, quaking in their eardrums, louder and louder until it seemed that what had exploded was there in the room on top of them in a blend of smashed, torn air, cries of the instantly dead, fall of steel, timber, and brick, crash of masonry and glass — they couldn't sort any of it out — all were there, all imaginable noises of destruction synthesized. It was like absolutely nothing they had ever heard before and it so filled their skulls, pushing outward from the brainpan, that they could not divide it into parts. All that they could understand, if they understood anything, was that this was the ultimate catastrophe, and that they were still recording it, expecting any second to be crushed into blackness, but as long as they were recording it they were still living. They felt, but did not think, this. They only understood it instinctively and held on tighter to each other, waiting for the smash, the crush, the black.

But it became lighter and lighter, the glow in the cellar room, waxing and intensifying itself. It had no color that they recognized through their tightly shut eyelids. It might have been called green, but it was not green, nor any neighbor of green. Like the noise, it was a dreadful compound of ultimately destructive fire, blast, terrible energy released from a bursting sun, like the birth of the solar system. Incandescence beyond an infinite number of lights swirled around them.

The worst was the nauseous rocking to and fro of the very earth beneath them, worse than an earthquake, which might have seemed reducible to human dimensions, those of some disaster witnessed in the movies or on television. But this was no gaping, opening seam in the earth, but a threatened total destruction of the earth itself, right to its core, a pulverization of the world. They tried like animals to scrabble closer and closer in under the north cellar wall even as they expected it to fall on them. They kept their heads down, waiting for death to take them as it had taken their friends, neighbors, fellow workers, policemen, firemen, soldiers; and the dreadful time passed and still they did not die in the catastrophe. And they began to sense obscurely that the longer they were left uncrushed, the better grew their chances of survival. And pitifully slowly their feelings began to resume their customary segmented play amongst themselves, while the event was still unfolding. They could not help doing the characteristic, the human, thing, the beginning to think and struggle to live.

Through their shut eyelids the light began to seem less incandescent, more recognizably a color familiar to human beings and less terrifying because it might be called a hue of green instead of no-color-at-all. It became green, still glowing and illuminating the cellar like daylight, but anyway green, nameable as such and therefore familiar and less dreadful. The light grew more and more darkly green in an insane harmony with the rocking and the sound.

As the rocking slowed, as they huddled closer and closer in under the north foundation, a split in the cellar wall showed itself almost in front of their hidden faces, and yet the wall stood and did not come in on top of them. It held and, holding, gave them more chance for survival although they didn't know it. The earth's upheaval slowed and sank back and no gaps appeared in the earth under them, no crevasse to swallow them up under the alteration of the earth's crust. And in time the rocking stopped and the floor of their world was still, but they would not move, afraid to move a limb for fear of being caught in the earth's mouth.

The noise continued, but began to distinguish itself in parts, and the worst basic element attenuated itself; that terrible crash apart of the atmosphere under the bomb had stopped by now, the atmosphere had parted to admit the ball of radioactivity, had been blown hundreds of miles in every direction, and had rushed back to regain its place, disputing that place with the ball of radioactivity, so that there grew up a thousand-mile vortex of cyclonic winds around the hub of the displacement. The cyclone was almost comforting, sounding, whistling, in whatever stood upright, not trees certainly, but tangled steel beams and odd bits of masonry. The sound of these winds came to them in the cellar. Soon they were able to name sounds, and distinguish them from others which they heard, mainly sounds of fire — no sounds of the dying, no human cries at all, no sounds of life. Only the fires and cyclonic winds.

Now they could feel, and hear enough to shout to each other over the fire and wind.

The man tried to stir, to ease his wife's position. He could move his torso so far as the waist or perhaps the hips. Below that, although he was in no pain and not paralyzed, he was immobilized by a heavy weight. He could feel his legs and feet; they were sound and unhurt, but he could not move them. He waited, lying there trying to sort things out, until some sort of ordered thought and some communication was possible, when the noise should lessen sufficiently. He could hear his wife shouting something into the dirt in front of her face and he tried to make it out.

"She slept through it," he heard, "she slept through it," and he couldn't believe it, although it was true. The baby lived and recollected none of the horror.

"She slept through it," screamed the wife idiotically, "she's still asleep." It couldn't be true, he thought, it was impossible, but there was no way to check her statement until they could move about. The baby must have been three feet below the blast and the glow, shielded by a two-and-a-half-foot wall of flesh, his and his wife's, and the additional thickness of layers of woollen clothing. She should certainly have survived, if they had, but how could she have slept through the noise, the awful light, and the rocking? He listened and waited, keeping his head down and his face covered.

Supposing that they had survived the initial blast, as seemed to be the case; there was still the fallout to consider. The likelihood, he thought (he was beginning to be able to think), was that they were already being eaten up by radiation and would soon die of monstrous cancers, or plain, simple leukemia, or rottenness of the cortex. It was miraculous that they had lived through the first shock; they could hardly hope that their luck would hold through the later dangers. He thought that the baby might not have been infected so far, shielded as she was, as he began to wonder how she might be helped to evade death from radiation in the next few days. Let her live a week, he thought, and she may go on living into the next generation, if there is one.

Nothing would be the same in the next generation; there would be few people and fewer laws, the national boundaries would have perished — there would be a new world to invent. Somehow the child must be preserved for that, even if their own lives were to be forfeited immediately. He felt perfectly healthy so far, untouched by any creeping sickness as he lay there, forcing himself and the lives beneath him deeper into their burrow. He began to make plans; there was nothing else for him to do just then.

The noise of the winds had become regular now and the green glow had subsided; the earth was still and they were still together and in the same place, in their cellar, in their home. He thought of his books, his checkbook, his phonograph records, his wife's household appliances. They were gone, of course, which didn't matter. What mattered was that the way they had lived was gone, the whole texture of their habits. The city would be totally uninhabitable. If they were to survive longer they must get out of the city at once. They would have to decide immediately when they should try to leave the city, and they must keep themselves alive until that time.

"What time is it?" gasped his wife from below him in a tone pitched in almost her normal voice. He was relieved to hear her speak in the commonplace, familiar tone; he had been afraid that hysteria and shock would destroy their personalities all at once. So far they had held together. Later on, when the loss of their whole world sank in, when they appreciated the full extent of their losses, they would run the risk of insanity or, at least, extreme neurotic disturbance. But right now they could converse, calculate, and wait for the threat of madness to appear days, or years, later.

He looked at his watch. "Eight-thirty," he said. Everything had ended in three and a half hours. "Are you all right?" he asked.

"I think so," she said, "I don't feel any pain and the baby's fine. She's warm and she doesn't seem frightened."

He tried to move his legs and was relieved to see that they answered the nervous impulse. He lifted his head fearfully and twisted it around to see behind him. His legs were buried under a pile of loose brick and rubble which grew smaller towards his thighs; his torso was quite uncovered. "I'm all right," he said, beginning to work his legs free; they were undoubtedly badly bruised, but they didn't seem to be crushed or broken; at the worst he might have torn muscles or a bad sprain. He had to be very careful, he reasoned, as he worked at his legs. He might dislodge something and bring the remnant of the house down around them. Very, very slowly he lifted his torso by doing a push-up with his arms. His wife slid out from underneath, pushing the baby in front of her.

When she was free she laid the child gently to one side, whispering to her and promising her food. She crawled around to her husband's side and began to push the bricks off his legs.

"Be careful," he whispered. "Take them as they come. Don't be in too much of a hurry."

She nodded, picking out the bricks gingerly, but as fast as she could. Soon he was able to roll over on his back and sit up. By a quarter to ten he was free and they took time to eat and drink. The three of them sat together in a cramped, narrow space under the cellar beams, perhaps six feet high and six or seven feet square. They were getting air from somewhere although it might be deadly air, and there was no smell of gas. He had been afraid that they might be suffocated in their shelter.

"Do you suppose the food's contaminated?" she asked.

"What if it is?" he said. "So are we, just as much as the food. There's nothing to do but risk it. Only be careful what you give the baby."

"How can I tell?"

"I don't know," he said. "Say a prayer and trust in God." He found the flashlight, which had rolled into a corner, and tried it. It worked very well.

"What are we going to do? We can't stay here."

"I don't even know for sure that we can get out," he said, "but we'll try. There should be a window just above us that leads to a crawl-space under the patio. That's one of the reasons why I told you to come here. In any case we'd be wise to stay here for a few hours until the very worst of the fallout is down."

"What'll we do when we get out?"

"Try to get out of town. Get our outer clothes off, get them all off for that matter, and scrub ourselves with water. Maybe we can get to the river."

"Why don't you try the window right now so we can tell whether we can get out?"

"I will as soon as I've finished eating and had a rest. My legs are very sore."

He could hear her voice soften. "Take your time," she said.

When he felt rested, he stood up. He could almost stand erect and with the flashlight was able to find the window quickly. It was level with his face. He piled loose bricks against the wall below it and climbed up on them until the window was level with his chest. Knocking out the screen with the butt of the flashlight, he put his head through and then flashed the light around; there were no obstructions that he could see, and he couldn't smell anything noxious. The patio, being a flat, level space, had evidently been swept clean by the blast without being flattened. They could crawl out of the cellar under the patio, he realized, and then kick a hole in the lath and stucco which skirted it.

He stepped down from the pile of brick and told his wife that they would be able to get out whenever they wished, that the crawl-space was clear.

"What time is it?"

"Half past twelve."

"Should we try it now?"

"I think so," he said. "At first I thought we ought to stay here for a day or two, but now I think we ought to try and get out from under the fallout. We may have to walk a couple of hundred miles."

"We can do it," she said and he felt glad. She had always been able to look unpleasant issues in the face.

He helped her through the cellar window and handed up the baby who clucked and chuckled when he spoke to her. He pushed the carton of food and the bucket of water after them. Then he climbed up and they inched forward under the patio.

"I hear a motor," said his wife suddenly.

He listened and heard it too.

"Looking for survivors," he said eagerly. "Probably the Army or Civil Defense. Come on."

He swung himself around on his hips and back and kicked

out with both feet at the lath and stucco. Three or four kicks did it. His wife went first, inching the baby through the hole. He crawled after her into the daylight; it looked like any other day except that the city was leveled. The sky and the light were the same; everything else was gone. They sat up, muddy, scratched, nervously exhausted, in a ruined flower bed. Not fifty feet away stood an olive-drab truck, the motor running loudly. Men shouted to them.

"Come on, you!" shouted the men in the truck. "Get going!" They stood and ran raggedly to the cab, she holding the child and he their remaining food and water. In the cab was a canvas-sheeted goggled driver, peering at them through huge eyes. "Get in the back," he ordered. "We've got to get out right away. Too hot." They climbed into the truck and it began to move instantly.

"Army Survival Unit," said a goggled and hooded man in the back of the truck. "Throw away that food and water; it's dangerous. Get your outer clothing off quick. Throw it out!" They obeyed him without thinking, stripping off their loose outer clothes and dropping them out of the truck.

"You're the only ones we've found in a hundred city blocks," said the soldier. "Did you know the war's over? There's a truce."

"Who won?"

"Over in half an hour," he said, "and nobody won."

"What are you going to do with us?"

"Drop you at a check-out point forty miles from here. Give you the scrub-down treatment, wash off the fallout. Medical check for radiation sickness. Clean clothes. Then we send you on your way to a refugee station.

"How many died?"

"Everybody in the area. Almost no exceptions. You're a statistic, that's what you are. Must have been a fluke of the blast."

"Will we live?"

"Sure you will. You're living now, aren't you?"

"I guess so," he said.

"Sure you'll live! Maybe not too long. But everybody else is dead! And you'll be taken care of." He fell silent.

They looked at each other, determined to live as long as they could. The wife cuddled the child close against her thin silk blouse. For a long time they jolted along over rocks and broken pavement without speaking. When the pavement smoothed out the husband knew that they must be out of the disaster area. In a few more minutes they were out of immediate danger; they had reached the check-out point. It was a quarter to three in the afternoon.

"Out you get," said the soldier. "We've got to go back." They climbed out of the truck and he handed down the baby. "You're all right now," he said. "Good luck."

"Good-bye," they said.

The truck turned about and drove away and they turned silently, hand in hand, and walked toward the medical tents. They were the seventh, eighth, and ninth living persons to be brought there after the sirens.

A VISIT TO THE FRONTIER
Ethel Wilson

Lucy turned from looking out of the window of the train.

The appearance of the country has changed since we left Saskatoon, hasn't it? she said, but Charles did not answer. He remained concealed by the weekend review which he was reading; so, since the question was of the kind which neither requires nor demands an answer, Lucy returned her gaze to the window.

Rivers flow through, or near, four of the five cities of the Canadian north and middle west. The fifth city, which has no large adjacent body of water, has courageously made itself a spacious lake in the dry prairies, and planted trees. The small northern city of Saskatoon on the high banks of the Saskatchewan River had given Lucy a great deal of pleasure. True, in summer the weather was very hot and in winter the weather was very cold. But the far spread of prairie, the vast span of sky with wildness of sunrise and sunset and aurora, the felt nearness of the northland, the grave majestic sweep of the tawny Saskatchewan River, the clarity and stimulation of the air delighted her — a dweller by the western ocean. So did the neatness of the heart of the small city; the dignity of the surprisingly large hotel upon the high river bank; the austere elegance of the large red brick churches on the river road, outlined clean against the clean sky as by some northern Canaletto; and those churches which terminated, also with elegance, in Byzantine onions.

By this time the train had left behind the flat prairies, and any suggestion of a town or even a dwelling was so improbable as to make one wonder, Will the curve of any small hill or valley here ever become home and significant and a part of memory to people who will live here and die here — all so empty of life now? (Yet see, a hawk!) Lucy sat wondering. The broad land slid behind them and now the country was broken, curved, into innumerable forested or bushy valleys and headlands, with stretches of intermediate green. Streams appeared around distant curves or near at hand, and vanished again, left behind. Was it the same stream? Were they many streams? And beyond the horizon disclosed by the speeding train, was there more of this softly moulded, recklessly planted and treed, mildly watered greenish brownish country, or did it change with suddenness into the true north? And what did the true north look like? she wondered. Perhaps this was the true north, momentarily kind, just before the end of autumn.

It is impossible to guess, so why guess, said Lucy, partly to herself and partly aloud and unheeded, whether this everlasting empty country will ever be settled with people and activity, will ever, in fact, be covered with towns and cities? We haven't seen a dwelling for hours. There are a great many factors of climate, water, soil, oil, minerals, transportation that must enter, of course. If you and I, two hundred years ago — which is nothing at all in time — should have found ourselves on the empty banks of the Saskatchewan River where Saskatoon now stands, we would have seen nothing to suggest the establishment of a town or city there, and the same is true now, and here.

A quiver of the weekend review caused Lucy to stop her soliloquy for the moment. There was nothing in what she had to say just then to warrant Charles's breaking off his reading and coming out of his private world to listen.

She turned her attention to him, and away from the window. How heavenly fortunate I am, she thought — and this time she kept her soliloquy to herself, as there are many things that do not translate into mutual speech and this was one — that ever since we first loved each other, every day has renewed our love. Never never have we taken it for granted but have always known, without saying, that it is our greatest thing and that it might be removed at any moment (although not in essence) by death, which comes once and forever to each person on earth, on this continent, on this train, and we are no exception. And so, now, as I sit across from Charlie and see him lounging there, and see his elbows sticking out each side of his paper, and his legs sprawled across, one boot touching my shoe, the contentment and joy of his presence is greater than when my heart first leapt to see him. And one wonders why most of the books that have ever been written and most of the tales that have been told (for the oldest tales were tales of fighting or of love) have been of nascent love, tragic love, deceived, faithless, or unlawful love, but not of perfect and lasting fulfilment. There is no literature of perfect and lasting fulfilment of happy love. That must be because continuing fulfilment does not lend itself to the curiosity that is impelled to read a story and because in any case this fulfilment can never be revealed.

Charles came out from behind the paper. Listen to this, he said, it's funny. He had come to the end of the paper where the competitions are. He read, and his French was pleasantly bad: "An English Member of Parliament who belonged to the M.R.A. related his confessions at a house party in France. He said '*Quand je regarde mon derrière, je vois qu'il est divisé en deux parties.*'" Lucy laughed a lot at this and at some similar stories in the competition, and Charles turned to the serious beginning of the review again and fell silent. Lucy now saw his face above the paper, intent and grown serious again.

The scenery had slipped behind the train unobserved, and the rather spectacular changes in the nature of the scenery had escaped Lucy's notice as she sat, still smiling at the derrière which was divisé. The roadbed appeared to be rough here and so the train gave the impression of hurrying. It was actually slower and rocked a good deal, and soap and glasses and bags and coats slipped and rattled and swayed in the compartment as the train ran on.

I'm glad, said Lucy out loud and still amused at the story, that now I've discovered —

Charles came up over the top of his paper again and looked at her. What on earth are you chunnering about now? he said.

I'm not chunnering, said Lucy. I'm simply saying — but she never said what she was simply saying because of the crash.

If it was a crash. It was a shattering, a physical impact, a screeching, a settling, a cessation in which she was seized and shaken and lost. It was for a millionth of a second — or forever — fear and helpless panic to the obliteration of

108

everything that had been Lucy. There was at last this settling down again to the irregular motion of the train and the assumption that something had happened and something was over. Lucy, who had so lately been in the middle of her laughing, had been banged about (it seemed), with sudden pain like thunder and lightning, and sat now with her eyes closed because she was afraid to open them. She remembered like a quick dream that once, in the sage-brush country, the train had run into a small herd of cattle. The train, at that time, had stopped, and there was a long wait while the poor beasts were removed from the rails. Evidently — and her first emotion was gladness — they had not run over anybody or any animal because they still kept on their way; probably one of the large boulders which so often overhang the railway cuttings had timed its falling to the vibrations of the train passing below and had knocked them about. Still a little fearful, Lucy opened her eyes and saw, but hazily, Charles sitting on the opposite seat, still reading. Really, Charlie, this is carrying imperturbability too far.

Darling, what was that? she said.

What was what? said Charles indifferently.

That crash, said his wife.

I don't know, said Charles and went on reading.

Sometimes you do infuriate me! said Lucy, and now I'm sure that you just pretend when you put it over me as you often do — being imperturbable like that. What *did* happen?

Charles looked up at her and the familiar look flowed between them. He said amiably, The train is slowing up. And it was.

Lucy still felt shaken. It's possible, she thought, that nothing happened at all, except inside my head. Dear me, I hope I'm not starting to have fits like a cat. Do people? she said out loud.

Do people what? asked Charles who had got up and was putting on his tweed jacket over his sweater.

Start having fits, she said.

At that moment the conductor put his head in at the

compartment door. Cut Off. This stop is Cut Off, he said. An hour and a half at Cut Off. You'll have time to go up to the settlement. They say it's worth seeing. And he went on and made his announcement along the train.

Lucy put on her leather jacket because they were pretty far north and the air would no doubt be nippy. They both went out.

She stepped on to the platform, glad to be free of the train for a long prospect of time, and stood before the sign of the railway station. The station was wooden, primitive, and so was the sign. It spelled CUT OFF . Lucy turned to the coloured porter who stood beside the steps. He was particularly nice and seemed to know the answers to all railroad questions.

Porter, she said, what an odd name. What does it mean?

The porter shrugged and regarded her with his slow gentle smile. Ah doan know, lady, he said. They's mighty odd names all over this country. They's The Leavings and Ah guess that kinda speaks for itself, n they's Dog Pound n Jumpn Pound n Ghost River n Spirit River but Ah doan know nuthn about Cut Off. Tell you the truth lady, it's the first time Ah done this run. And he helped down another passenger.

The air was brilliantly fresh after the train smell. Lucy breathed deep. She noticed the passenger who had followed them off the train. He was tall. His face was serious and perhaps sad. He regarded his surroundings with slow sweeping glances which were also inward glances and he appeared anxious.

Who's that, Charles? breathed Lucy. I've seen him or seen his picture and why is he so sad?

That is Proker, said Charles, and he has lost his fountain pen. Perhaps he lost it when we changed trains.

Changed trains? said Lucy. (Changed trains *changed trains changed trains* changed trains.) Her head clanged. She put her hand to her eyes, closing them, and then it was better and she stepped out with Charlie because they had no time to waste.

They left behind the little wooden station and the people standing about and walked into the open space to see what

110

they could of the settlement of Cut Off.

Impressions flowed in on Lucy like a newly tasted wine, and yet taste was the only faculty unemployed. Simultaneously, simultaneously, they flowed in, ravishing her. The prospect revealed itself to the north towards which they looked as an open stretch of brisk grass in front of them, crossed by paths and wagon trails and sloping down to a near river which cut foaming across the landscape. This river which was large enough to be spectacular and powerful and yet not useful for navigation was of water so whitely brilliant as to be quite dazzling in its motion. It had a strange peculiarity which Lucy had never seen before in picture or story; and now she marvelled that this attribute of the river had not already become famous. At intervals in the course of the river, both on its banks and springing up through the waters of the river itself, were fountains, rising buoyantly and joyously several feet in the air. Only to look at these fountains of bright perpetual water refreshed and revived Lucy — and perhaps other watchers too, for some of the other passengers were standing, gazing — so that her sense of well-being was beyond anything she had ever felt before. They stood, and then looked beyond the river, where lay the settlement proper. The river was crossed by two simple wooden bridges that led to the settlement.

Wood seemed to be abundant here. Spreading trees which still held their leaves and large dark comely firs and shapely cedars grew, not very crowded, on either side of the sloping river banks. Indians and other people walked here, separately or together, or stood looking at the fountains of springing waters, or sat upon the pine- and cedar-scented earth. A look to right and left showed the country folded away and away further and further into hills and valleys behind hills and valleys, wild yet embowered in trees; away until soft brown and green hills of wiry tawny grass and light and dark trees became dun-coloured, mauve, and then deeply purple. Lucy turned back to look at the river. Across the river flew one after another of small western blue-birds, bluer than forget-me-nots

111

in flight, and there came continuous bird-song from the trees.

She was soon aware that the air which they were breathing was different from the air she customarily breathed and whose quality she used not to notice particularly unless it was exceptionally bad. This air, at Cut Off, was vigorous, so vigorous that Lucy felt herself different, stronger, and gayer. She said to Charles, Don't you feel as if the air we used to breathe was more like earth and stone than air — solid and heavy, I mean — and I feel as if it was only water that I used to have in my veins. This must be the true north.

But Charles did not answer.

She turned and looked up but he was not there. She looked back. Perhaps he had gone to hunt for the fountain pen. Or was it possible — but not likely — that Charles had walked on alone or with some other people?

Charles! Darling! Charlie! she called, but he cannot have heard her.

Well, she thought, how strange, but he must have gone on ahead. I'll hurry after, I mustn't wait here, we'll meet at the train. She found it much easier than usual not to worry. She was aware as she walked on quickly, and with a delight in walking, that she had shed some accompanying emotion (the emotion was anxiety). Even the unaccountable absence of Charles did not make her anxious.

This delicious air, strong and pine-scented, which she drew in gave her active pleasure. It *was* like water or wine compared to earth or stone. She came to the nearer footbridge and stood for a few moments watching the lively river and the strange crystalline fountains that shot vertically upwards and sprayed down again into the rushing sparkling stream whose noise was strangely agreeable. She watched, too, some of the people who seemed to be inhabitants enjoying the river and its banks. These people walked quickly, or strolled, or sat on the ground. But whether they walked or wandered or rested, whether moving or in repose, there was a lively look of well-being and pleasure upon them. They talked to each other in passing and laughed spontaneously. Even a crippled man whom she saw making his way on crutches by the river bank seemed to swing along in an easy debonair fashion and whistled as he swung. They feel as I do, thought Lucy; this is certainly a very healthy place.

On the footbridge as she stopped to look down at the water racing radiant and broken under the bridge, a man and woman leaned upon the railing. Lucy heard them talking and found that their language was strange to her; but she had a vague sentiment of knowing what they were talking about, although she did not understand the words, only the feeling. They looked at her in friendly fashion and seemed as if they would include her in the conversation only that they knew she could not converse with them. Lucy wondered if this were one of the many foreign settlements to be found in the Canadian northwest — Ukrainians, Hutterites. No, not Hutterites; these people had no uniformity of dress.

She realized that time (was it time?) was passing, and that if she were to climb the far slope and see the buildings which the trees partly disclosed, she could no longer stand there water-gazing. So she crossed the footbridge, and leaving the river bank she climbed the gradual slope of the hill, following a trail which led up among the trees.

She felt no shortness of breath, as she sometimes did, but an increased exhilaration in this climbing. People in twos and threes climbed, too, or walked down the hill and towards the river. She was struck by the freedom and elasticity of their steps, and the certainty and serenity of their faces. They were not like the crowds she knew. She did not recognize the absence of anxiety or preoccupation in them or in herself, because there was no anxiety to recognize. This is a country of truth! she thought, surprised. We are free like birds.

She now saw through the trees, which had become fewer, a long low building of dark stained rough wood. The building was pleasing in its simple proportions. There was a long verandah which faced west. The settlement of Cut Off must be unexpectedly large, she thought, for already she had seen more people than would usually constitute a village, and she found

113

that more were coming and going in and out of the unusually large doors of the building which was perhaps some kind of lodge or village centre. As she went up to the broad, shallow, wooden steps towards the entrance, she saw that there were, higher up the trail, other buildings among the trees. Is there a church? she wondered. If I could see a church, that would tell me something.

She was about to cross the theshold of the lodge quite eagerly, without any customary shyness, and to mingle with the people amongst whom friendliness seemed to blow like a breeze — although no-one appeared to notice her — when there sounded the very loud ringing of a bell. She turned quickly. Something in her spirit and spirits descended and became confused, and she remembered the time, and the train, and above all she remembered Charles. Without looking further inside the lodge she went with an attempt at haste down the hill. So far from buoying her up as the bright air had heretofore done, the bright air was too strong for her and now pressed her down, so that she made her way with some difficulty until she reached a low rectangular stone, seat high. She looked down upon the stone, and on it was chiselled a finely sweeping double curve. She bent down and followed this curve with her finger, murmuring The Line of Beauty, The Line of Beauty. She thought, I must sit down for a moment on this stone for I am very tired and I am confused. So she sank down and sat on the stone, and looked towards the dazzling jets of water which no longer invigorated her but were far too strong, as some strong drink might be too strong. A man walked up to her and stood over her, and she looked up at him and was grateful for something in his face. He spoke to her, and although she could not understand his words she knew that he wished to be kind. I am like a dog who is lost, she thought, and he is like a man who is kind to the dog and powerful; but because he is a man and I am a dog, however kind and powerful he is, we cannot communicate except on the level of pity. He helped her to rise, and she hurried on, labouring as she ran.

114

After she crossed the footbridge, her mind and body freshened a little, and some of her calm and pleasure seemed to be restored, so that she did not race and press on to the railway station with anxiety. There were new sounds in the air. She heard from her right, behind the brow of a curving hill, the galloping of hooves. And there was this peculiarity in this air, that one sound did not overlay or drown out another sound; so that the sound of galloping hooves which drew nearer and nearer did not at all drown the sound of light and laughing voices calling to one another.

Around the curve swept into view, one, two, seven, twelve horses and their riders. Lucy stood entranced.

The girls who raced their horses round the concealing curve of the hill, into the clearing, and across the clearing to a spinney of thin trees, turned to each other as they galloped, and seemed to be in a kind of laughing harmony. They wore bright scarves which fluttered behind them in the wind; so that these merry riders galloping towards the spinney with their bright scarves flowing behind them were a beautiful sight. The heavy hooves pounded, the gay voices sounded, the scarves streamed and fluttered, all in the brilliant air. Lucy stood like a radiant statue, watching. When the riders reached the spinney, they slid down off their horses, while the sound of their light voices crossed and criss-crossed. They threw the reins forward over their horses' heads and the horses stood, tossing their long manes, switching their tails, and moving only a step or two towards a patch of grass or a green bough.

Lucy was so enchanted with the girl riders that she had again forgotten her urgency. Some of the girls wore full divided skirts such as a riding gypsy might wear (but they were not gypsies), and walking lightly, talking and laughing together, they set out quickly for the footbridge by which Lucy had just crossed the river, some in blue jeans, some in gypsy skirts, all with their scarves fluttering. One bright-eyed Indian girl saw Lucy standing there and waved to her as they passed. Lucy waved back, very much pleased at this. Where do they come from behind those hills? What is it, there? Why do they come? But the girls had gone towards the bridge and only the horses remained in the spinney, resting, pawing, and shaking their heads. Lucy heard again the loud station bell. The train was pulling out. Oh! she gasped and began to run.

She ran, and caught a handle beside a step; a hand from a dark blue sleeve clutched her and she swung onto the train.

Oh thank you, she gasped to the conductor, and made her way into the train. There was no-one there. The train was very old. Not a single passenger. There was no sign at all that Charles had ever been there. It was not the same train. Oh! she cried desperately, and found her way to the conductor. I'm on the wrong train! Where is my husband?

The conductor said You must have changed trains (changed trains *changed trains changed trains* changed trains).

If you want to get off, said the conductor, you'd better jump before the train gets up speed. Her one desire was to get off. She stood on the lowest step of this old-fashioned train, still holding on and — divided between the desire to leave the train at once before it got up speed, and the desire to choose a good place on which to jump out so that she would not disable herself — she jumped, onto a soft grassy mound. She scrambled up, and in raising herself she leaned her weight on a soft but firm object that moved beneath her hand. She looked down in a hurry and saw that her hand rested upon the flat head of a large polar bear. She drew her hand away in alarm, but not before she had felt the texture of the crisp, coarse, gleaming, cream-coloured hair. The bear looked at her with humourless animal eyes and extended its head this way that way — this way, that way — and then paid her no attention. She thought as she regained her equilibrium and started to run the short distance back to the station. Yes, this must be the true north, yet something is wrong about that bear.

And as she ran she began to be aware that living in this country would, of itself, inescapably exclude the memory of much sorrow and much joy that made up the uneven fabric of her life as she had known it. She began to pray as she ran, panting, stumbling. Oh God just this. Let me find him. Where is he? Let me find him. Just to be together. Only that. Oh God, oh God!

When she reached the station she saw that their own train was beside the little platform. She stood and scanned the windows anxiously. There, looking out of a window was the serious face of the passenger who had lost his fountain pen. She mounted the steps and hurried to their compartment. Charles was not there. The weekend review lay upon the seat where he had put it down. For some reason she clutched the paper and held it tightly crumpled in her hand. She made her way down the car — the train had begun to move — to where their fellow-passenger sat. She supported herself at his open compartment door.

Please, she said to the poet — for she felt somehow that he was a poet or kin to a poet — have you seen my husband? I have lost him.

I saw him, said the passenger, but he is not here now. He came back to the train and looked for you. He told me, She always likes water and she must have followed the river. So he took the far footbridge and followed down the stream. I am very sorry, said the passenger deliberately and with compassion.

Lucy turned and went back with great difficulty to the steps. It seemed as though she fell, and lay there, on the tawny prairie.

In the course of time, or of time and a time, all memory and strange pictures and confusion of human experience left her, and she died.

When those who were killed in the train wreck had at last recovered from the fatigues of death, it may be that some of them met again with a transfigured delight in that beautiful and happy country, with death past and over. We do not know.

QUESTIONS ON THE THEME:
The Frontier Experience

1. Choose a local scene which has impressed you as particularly interesting or unique. Imagine you are the first person to see it and write a descriptive passage intended for someone who has never been there. Try to appeal to the reader's senses and to imply your own feelings about the place rather than stating them directly.
2. Write a fictitious diary entry for a day in the life of a pioneer in the area close to your home. Some research may first be necessary into the daily life of pioneers in your community.
3. Spend some time talking to a person who "pioneered" in your district or somewhere near. Record some of these impressions and be prepared to compare his/her experiences with those encountered in this book.
4. Write a short passage, in prose or poetry, expressing your feelings when completely alone.
5. Visit a park or a wilderness area with a notebook and describe what you discover. Do not be content with generalizations; put your nose up close and examine the concrete details which can make for interesting writing.
6. Examine a map of Canada closely. Find place names which sound intriguing. Find the areas which have the sparsest population. Note the main geographical regions of the country and for each discover what are the most obvious features of its landscape, the most likely dangers of its wilderness areas, the most pleasurable aspects of what it offers. Discuss, if you can, the reasons for the locations of the most heavily populated areas. Which of all these regions would you best like to explore? For a region not your own, find out who are its best-known writers and do a little reading. Write a short essay telling why you would like to explore that region. Write a short narrative in which a person from that region first encounters your region.
7. Relate an actual experience you have had (as witness or as participant) to one of the kinds of frontier experience represented in this book. Use it as a basis or source of inspiration to create an "artistic experience" to share with the reader. Using the short story, essay, or poetic form, select and

arrange and invent your material to shape a piece of writing that gives you satisfaction and gives the reader some sense of the experience's significance.

8. The following are quotations from prominent Canadian literary critics. For each, find supportive examples amongst the selections in this text. Then, discuss the relevance or truth of each quotation with your classmates.

   (a) To speak the language of "West" is not to be merely regional in bias . . . but to articulate the tension between order and disorder, myth and reality, that underlies Canadian writing. (W.H. New: *Articulating West*)

   (b) The fugitive, solitude and wilderness, romance and moral drama, the search for meaning, these characterize the frontier effect in Canadian literature of exile. (John Moss: *Patterns of Isolation*)

   (c) Canadian writers as a whole do not trust Nature; they are always suspecting some dirty trick. (Margaret Atwood: *Survival*)

   (d) The real terror comes when the individual feels himself becoming an individual, pulling away from the group, losing the sense of driving power that the group gives him, aware of a conflict within himself far subtler than the struggle of morality against evil. (Northrop Frye: "Conclusion" in Klinck: *A Literary History of Canada*)

9. The general tone of most selections in this book is fairly grim. Can you see reasons for this? Can you, through further reading, find examples of frontier writing which are less pessimistic?

10. Find and read other writings by the author of the selection in this book which interested you the most. Is the selection in this book consistent in attitude and approach with his other work? Does the frontier appear as a significant element in his other work?

11. As a class project you might consider producing a supplement to this book for a future class to use, including both student writing and the works of writers in your province who have dealt with the frontier theme. Before doing so, examine closely the thematic structure of this anthology, and consider the reasons for the inclusion of each of the selections as well as for the order in which they are arranged.

BIBLIOGRAPHY

BIOGRAPHICAL INFORMATION

Carl F. Klinck, *A Literary History of Canada: Canadian Literature in English*, University of Toronto Press

Norah Story, *The Oxford Companion to Canadian History and Literature*, Oxford University Press

William Stewart Wallace, *The Macmillan Dictionary of Canadian Biography*, Macmillan of Canada

CRITICAL WORKS

Margaret Atwood, *Survival*, Anansi

Northrop Frye, *The Bush Garden*, Anansi

D. G. Jones, *Butterfly on Rock*, University of Toronto Press

John Moss, *Patterns of Isolation*, McClelland & Stewart

W. H. New, *Articulating West*, New Press

Elizabeth Waterston, *Survey: A Short History of Canadian Literature*, Methuen

POETRY

Margaret Atwood, *The Journals of Susanna Moodie*; *The Animals in That Country*, Oxford University Press

George Bowering, *Rocky Mountain Foot*, McClelland & Stewart

Earle Birney, "David" in *Selected Poems*, McClelland & Stewart

Ralph Gustafson, *Rocky Mountain Poems,* McClelland & Stewart

Dennis Lee, *Civil Elegies and Other Poems,* Anansi

Douglas LePan, "Coureur de Bois" in *The Book of Canadian Poetry*, A. J. M. Smith, ed., Gage

Gwendolyn MacEwen, *The Shadow Maker*, Macmillan of Canada

John Newlove, *Black Night Window*, McClelland & Stewart

Michael Ondaatje, *The Collected Works of Billy the Kid*, Anansi

E. J. Pratt, "Brébeuf and His Brethren", "Towards the Last Spike" in *The Collected Poems of E. J. Pratt*, Macmillan of Canada

Al Purdy, *North of Summer*; *Selected Poems*, McClelland & Stewart

Frank R. Scott, "Laurentian Shield", "Northern Stream" in *Selected Poems*, Oxford University Press

Robert Service, *Songs of a Sourdough,* McGraw-Hill Ryerson

J. Michael Yates, *The Great Bear Lake Meditations*, Oberon

SHORT STORIES

Matt Cohen, "Columbus and the Fat Lady" in *Columbus and the Fat Lady*, Anansi

Hugh Garner, "The Moose and the Sparrow" in *Men and Women*, Simon and Schuster

Frederick Philip Grove, "Snow" in *A Book of Canadian Stories*, Desmond Pacey, ed., McGraw-Hill Ryerson

Hugh Hood, "Getting to Williamstown" in *The Fruit Man, the Meat Man, and the Manager*, Oberon

Malcolm Lowry, "The Forest Path to the Spring" in *Hear Us O Lord from Heaven Thy Dwelling Place*, McClelland & Stewart

Sinclair Ross, "The Lamp at Noon" in *The Lamp at Noon and Other Stories*, McClelland & Stewart

Wallace Stegner, "Carrion Spring" in *Wolf Willow*, Macmillan of Canada

NON-FICTION

Pierre Berton, *The National Dream; The Last Spike*, McClelland & Stewart

Emily Carr, *Hundreds and Thousands*, Clarke, Irwin

Eric Collier, *Three Against the Wilderness*, Clarke, Irwin

Kildare Dobbs, *Running to Paradise*, PaperJacks

Alan Fry, *Come a Long Journey*, Doubleday

Grey Owl, *Tales of an Empty Cabin*, Macmillan of Canada

Richmond P. Hobson, Jr., *Grass Beyond the Mountains*, McClelland & Stewart

Thomas P. Kelley, *The Rat River Trapper*, PaperJacks

Nellie McClung, *Clearing in the West*, Thomas Allen

Susanna Moodie, *Roughing It in the Bush*, McClelland & Stewart; *Life in the Clearings*, Macmillan of Canada

Farley Mowat, *Tundra*, McClelland & Stewart

Jack Paterson, *Cranberry Portage*, McClelland & Stewart

Catherine Parr Traill, *The Backwoods of Canada*, Coles

NOVELS

Frances Moore Brooke, *The History of Emily Montague*, McClelland & Stewart

Philip Child, *The Village of Souls*, McGraw-Hill Ryerson

Ralph Connor, *The Man from Glengarry*, McClelland & Stewart
Wayland Drew, *The Wabeno Feast*, Anansi
Alan Fry, *The Revenge of Annie Charlie*, Doubleday
Martin Grainger, *Woodsmen of the West*, McClelland & Stewart
Frederick Philip Grove, *The Fruits of the Earth*, McClelland &
    Stewart
Howard O'Hagan, *Tay John*, New Canadian Library
Robert Harlow, *Scann*, Sono Nis
Harold Horwood, *White Eskimo*, Doubleday
Robert Kroetsch, *But We Are Exiles*, Macmillan of Canada
Frederick Niven, *The Flying Years*, New Canadian Library
John Richardson, *Wacousta,* McClelland & Stewart
Ringuet, *Thirty Acres*, McClelland & Stewart
Gabrielle Roy, *The Hidden Mountain*, New Canadian Library
Robert J. C. Stead, *Grain*, McClelland & Stewart
Paul St. Pierre, *Breaking Smith's Quarter Horse*, McGraw-Hill
    Ryerson

FILMS
All available from the National Film Board

Feature Films
Cry of the Wild, colour, 88 minutes
Drylanders, black and white, 69 minutes

Documentaries
The Best Damn Fiddler from Calabogie to Kaladär, black and white,
    49 minutes
A Crowded Wilderness, colour, 9 minutes
Fort Who?, colour, 10 minutes
Mudflats Living, colour, 28 minutes
North, colour, 14 minutes
Pangnirtung, colour, 29 minutes
Yukon Old, Yukon New, colour, 19 minutes

57   67   77   87   97   08   18   28   38 THB 9   8   7   6   5   4   3   2   1